ON THEIR SHOULDERS

The Women Who Paved the Way in Nova Scotia Politics

GRACE EVANS & SARAH DOBSON

On Their Shoulders
Copyright © 2021 by Grace Evans & Sarah Dobson

All rights reserved. No part of this publication may be reproduced, distributed, or transmitted in any form or by any means, including photocopying, recording, or other electronic or mechanical methods, without the prior written permission of the author, except in the case of brief quotations embodied in critical reviews and certain other non-commercial uses permitted by copyright law.

Tellwell Talent
www.tellwell.ca

ISBN
978-0-2288-4501-0 (Hardcover)
978-0-2288-4500-3 (Paperback)
978-0-2288-4502-7 (eBook)

"If I have seen further, it is by standing on the shoulders of giants."

—*Isaac Newton*

TABLE OF CONTENTS

FOREWORD vii
THIS BOOK ix
NOTE FROM THE AUTHORS.. xi

1. GLADYS PORTER 1
2. MELINDA MACLEAN, QC, BARRISTER & SOLICITOR (RET'D) 3
3. ALEXA MCDONOUGH, OC, ONS... 6
4. THE HONOURABLE MAXINE COCHRAN 9
5. CORA ETTER 12
6. THE HONOURABLE SANDY JOLLY 14
7. THE HONOURABLE MARIE DECHMAN 16
8. THE HONOURABLE FRANCENE COSMAN 19
9. LILA O'CONNOR 22
10. THE HONOURABLE ELEANOR NORRIE 25
11. EILEEN O'CONNELL 28
12. HELEN MACDONALD 30
13. THE HONOURABLE MAUREEN MACDONALD 34
14. YVONNE ATWELL 38
15. ROSEMARY GODIN 41
16. MARY ANN MCGRATH 44
17. THE HONOURABLE JANE PURVES 47
18. MURIEL BAILLIE 50
19. JOAN MASSEY 52
20. THE HONOURABLE MARILYN MORE 53
21. MICHELE RAYMOND 57
22. THE HONOURABLE DIANA WHALEN 60
23. THE HONOURABLE CAROLYN BOLIVAR GETSON 64
24. THE HONOURABLE JUDY STREATCH 67
25. THE HONOURABLE KAREN CASEY 70
26. VICKI CONRAD 72

27. BECKY KENT	76
28. THE HONOURABLE KELLY REGAN	80
29. THE HONOURABLE DENISE PETERSON-RAFUSE	83
30. THE HONOURABLE RAMONA JENNEX	86
31. PAM BIRDSALL	89
32. LENORE ZANN	92
33. JOYCE TREEN	97
34. THE HONOURABLE JOANNE BERNARD	100
35. THE HONOURABLE PATRICIA ARAB	103
36. THE HONOURABLE LENA METLEGE DIAB	105
37. THE HONOURABLE MARGARET MILLER	108
38. THE HONOURABLE SUZANNE LOHNES-CROFT	111
39. KARLA MACFARLANE	113
40. PAM EYKING	116
41. MARIAN MANCINI	119
42. LISA ROBERTS	120
43. TAMMY MARTIN	123
44. ALANA PAON	125
45. RAFAH DICOSTANZO	126
46. BARBARA ADAMS	128
47. ELIZABETH SMITH-MCCROSSIN	132
48. SUSAN LEBLANC	134
49. CLAUDIA CHENDER	136
50. KIM MASLAND	139
ACKNOWLEDGEMENTS	143
PHOTOGRAPAHY	145
SPONSORS	147
ABOUT THE AUTHORS	149

FOREWORD

Nova Scotia elected its first representative government in 1758. It was over 200 years later that the first woman, Gladys Porter, would take her seat at Province House. In fact, women would not have the right to vote until 1920—162 years after the first government sat.

Women were actually not specifically excluded from voting between 1758–1851, and there is some evidence that a handful of women did cast votes during that time. However, in 1851, legislation was passed that explicitly excluded women from the vote. It would not be until 1918 that women were allowed to vote if they were property owners, and then 1920 when some women in Nova Scotia got the vote devoid of property conditions.

In 1918, some women also gained the right to run for office. The first women put their names on a ballot in 1929. Grace McLeod Rogers and Bertha A. Donaldson were the first two women in the province of Nova Scotia brave enough to run for provincial government. It would take forty years, and six more women running and losing, before Gladys Porter's successful campaign in 1960.

In Nova Scotia's electoral history, there have been exactly fifty women to be a Member of the Legislative Assembly (MLA).[1] This book is dedicated to telling their stories. As of the writing in 2020, seven of those women have passed away. Sixteen women are currently serving, and thirty-two of the women elected to the legislature were elected after the year 2000.

Gladys Porter served from her 1960 election until her death in 1967. The next woman to take her seat in the legislature was Melinda MacLean in 1974. After she departed politics in 1978, Alexa McDonough followed in 1981. She served until 1993, ensuring that there was never again a time there were no female voices in the Nova Scotia Legislature. She was also the first female party leader in Nova Scotia, taking leadership of the New Democratic Party in 1980.

In 1985, Maxine Cochran became the first woman to take her place around the cabinet table, as Minister of Transportation. She also served as Minister of Consumer Affairs, Minister of Culture, Recreation, and Fitness, and Minister responsible for the Advisory Council on the Status of Women. Since Maxine, there have been twenty women to serve in cabinet positions.

Marie Dechman was appointed the first female Minister of Community Services in 1991. She was also the first deputy Speaker of the House, being appointed to the position in 1989. Jane Purves became the first female Minister of Education in 1999, as well as the first female Minister of Health in 2002.

It was not until 2012 that Nova Scotia had its first female Minister of Finance, when Maureen MacDonald took the position. And even more recently, Lena Metlege Diab became the first female Minister of Justice and Attorney General of Nova Scotia in 2013. Diana Whalen became the first female deputy premier that same year.

As of the writing of this book, Nova Scotia has not had a female Speaker of the legislature. We are also one of four provinces to have never had a female premier.

---

[1] Right before the submission of *On Their Shoulders,* the fifty-first woman was elected to the Nova Scotia Legislature. Kendra Coombes was elected MLA for Cape Breton Centre on March 10, 2020.

THIS BOOK

This book began as an idea for a fundraiser. We wanted to raise money to start a scholarship that could help women dreaming of a political career, and selling a book seemed like an appropriate way to raise funds. We thought it would be a fun and easy idea to have the fifty women to ever serve as MLA profiled in the book.

But it has become so much more.

When we contacted the women, we realized no one had ever undertaken a project like this before—to record the history of Nova Scotian provincial politics from a female perspective, and with a gendered lens. As we began interviews, we realized we were taking on a project that would become much larger than just a simple fundraising idea. It quickly became evident how important this project was to the women involved in it, and to women generally. So what began as a fun, fast fundraiser turned into a much more involved, and much more important, project.

We always maintained that we wanted this book to be a way for women to tell their stories in their own words. We interviewed and recorded the words of the women who were willing to meet with us and tell their stories, and all of the excerpts you find in this book were kept in those original words. While some might expect a more factual version of this history, this book is about more than just recording dates and names. It was an opportunity for women to tell their own personal and political history. Really, this book is the result of women finally being asked: *what is your story?*

We were lucky enough to get to travel the province and speak to almost all of the women to serve as MLA, or the families of those who have passed away. We asked them to tell their stories—their background, what led them to running for office, what barriers they faced as a woman, what they are most proud of in their life and what advice they would have for young women entering politics. Being that these are the words of the fifty women profiled; we feel it must be noted that this book is not a record of fact. Stories in this book were not corroborated or fact checked. They are reflective of the perspective of the woman telling them.

This book became both a reflection on women in politics, and also a reflection on how politics is done in Nova Scotia. It is our belief that there are many positive stories in this book. But there are also many places where you will see women calling for change. A call for more collaboration, less division between parties, more kindness on social media and on the floor of the legislature. A call for both men and women to make room around the table for more diverse voices.

As we believe you will read, almost everyone runs for politics with a desire to help their community and to change the province for the better. Despite the way our system sometimes makes it feel, we all have the same goal. We hope this book serves as a reminder to all elected officials, and all who hope to run for office, on the importance of their roles and to always remember why they were called to public office in the first place.

NOTE FROM THE AUTHORS

In the making of this project, we read something Sarah Dobson (co-author) said in an interview in 2017, while a political science student at Dalhousie University:

"There is a self-doubt that [women] go into politics with—can I aspire to the highest office? Can I be prime minister? Is there a point of taking this path if I can only ever reach 70 percent of the height of politics?"[2]

While we created this book and spoke to the women who have served in this province, we realized that the women contained in these pages were those who were brave enough to trek forward without an answer to those questions. They were the ones who were willing, despite that doubt, to try to find a place for women's voices in our province. They did so knowing they might not reach the top—willing to accept the disappointment, sadness, and anger that comes with forging a path in a place you are told you do not belong.

And we realized that the path that we, and so many others, are walking today was forged relentlessly by them and everyone who supported them. Every brick that we walk with ease today was laid by a woman who had to fight for her place, who had to push for every inch gained. We have never been more aware that we follow still along the path they are making. If the end of that path is equity, the chance to lead and be equal, then they are still paving our way there.

We hope that these stories can shed some light on who these women are, and we hope it is clear that their stories are not just about gender. Men's stories are not inherently tied to their gender, and nor should ours be. These are words spoken by these women about what inspires them, what led them to politics, what disappoints them, what they are proud of, and what they would say to those who come next.

This book is both a celebration, and a highlight of failure. It is both a record of how far we have come, and a statement on how far we have to go. You can learn as much from whose stories are contained in these pages as you can from whose are not. This book is meant to be read with admiration for those stories it contains, but also with solidarity for the many women whose stories are still being silenced.

We sincerely hope that there will be a sequel to this book with the stories of the next fifty elected women. And we hope that the sequel takes fewer than 200 years to be written.

---

[2] Prevail, Sean. "'Took My Breath away': Halifax woman reflects on Daughters of the Vote." March 14, 2017. https://globalnews.ca/news/3303589/took-my-breath-away-halifax-woman-reflects-on-daughters-of-the-vote/

Sarah and Grace looking at the wall filled with portraits of past premiers at the Nova Scotia Legislature - a wall filled entirely with white men.

Photo courtesy of Nova Scotia Legislature

1. GLADYS PORTER (1893 – 1967)
PC MLA FOR KINGS NORTH 1960–1967

Gladys Porter was a trailblazer in Nova Scotia politics. As the first woman to run for mayorship of any town in the Maritimes, she defeated her male opponent and became the mayor of Kentville, Nova Scotia, in 1946. For eleven years, Gladys continued to serve as mayor before putting her name forward as the Progressive Conservative candidate for Kings North in 1960. Yet again, Gladys set an important precedent as she became the first female member of the legislative assembly in Nova Scotia.

As the daughter of a seven-term mayor in Sydney, Cape Breton, Gladys was no stranger to the political world. Throughout her life, Gladys was a tireless advocate for women's rights. She often faced significant vitriol for her work in what had been an entirely male-dominated environment until her arrival. In fact, during her mayoral campaign, Gladys told voters not to vote for or against her as a woman, but rather to vote for her as a human being. She never let the opinions of others interfere in her important work as she persisted to advocate for children's issues, healthcare, and women in business.

Gladys's devotion to her community was evident in everything she did. A local newspaper, *The Register*, writes of the night Gladys won her first term as mayor of Kentville in 1946. The results of the election were set to come in, but rather than waiting to hear the outcome, Gladys went to teach a cooking class at the Kentville Evening Technical Class—a role she had held for quite some time. No matter the events in her personal life, she never wavered in her commitment to the town of Kentville, and eventually the riding of Kings North.

During her time as MLA, Gladys was able to obtain provincial funding to construct a bridge connecting Greenwich and Port Williams. It was completed in 1968—a year after her death. More than forty years later, in 2010, the Department of Transportation renamed the bridge after her, paying homage to Gladys's legacy.

More information about the life and legacy of Gladys Porter can be found at the Kings County Museum, where a section is dedicated to her. Her portrait continues to be the only woman featured on the floor of the Nova Scotia Legislature at the time of publication.[3]

---

[3] This section is drawn from Saltwire Network "Kentville's Gladys Porter a political pioneer." October 26, 2016. https://www.saltwire.com/lifestyles/kentvilles-gladys-porter-a-political-pioneer-71887/

2. MELINDA MACLEAN, QC, Barrister & Solicitor (ret'd)
LIBERAL SENIOR MEMBER FOR COLCHESTER COUNTY 1974–1978

In April 1974, I was elected as a Liberal Member to the Nova Scotia Legislature for the dual constituency of Colchester County.[4] I was twenty-eight years of age, the only female elected at that time (the second in the province's history) and my title in the House was Senior Member for Colchester County, having received more votes in the election than the other five candidates who offered. I served one term from 1974 to 1978 and did not reoffer.

However, in 1974, I had no plans to run for office. At that time, I was practicing law in Truro for Nova Scotia Legal Aid, the first female to practice law in Colchester County. I had previously practiced law in Sydney, where the Nova Scotia Legal Aid office first opened there in late 1972.

In the spring of 1974, when the election was called by the governing Liberals, Colchester County was represented by two prominent Progressive Conservatives, both of whom were cabinet ministers in the previous Conservative administrations. In March 1974, two candidates for the Liberal Party had already offered for nomination. However, to generate interest for the election in the constituency, the Liberal Party wanted a third candidate to ensure that the nomination convention was a contested one. My father was well known as a Liberal, a lawyer, later a judge, who had represented Colchester County

---

[4] At the time, Colchester County was a dual riding. Voters are given the opportunity to vote for two candidates. They typically vote for two candidates from the same party.

from 1945 to 1949. Thereafter, the constituency had been a Conservative stronghold for twenty-five years.

I was approached to put my name forward as the desired 'third candidate.'

I agreed, having no reason to believe that the convention would nominate anyone other than the two established, willing candidates who were already campaigning for the two positions available on the Liberal ticket. Furthermore, there was no reason to believe that the Liberals would necessarily win. Both men were nominated at the convention, but the vote was close, with the 'third candidate' just four votes behind. I was not dismayed as I had offered only as an accommodation to the party, for I was thoroughly engaged in my law practice.

However, things changed dramatically during the short campaign. Health considerations required one of the two nominated Liberals to withdraw, and, there being no time to convene a second convention, I was in effect 'drafted' to fill the vacancy by the local Liberal Association, which by then was determined to win the constituency if at all possible.

Although it had not appeared at all likely, after twenty-five years of Conservative representation, the people of Colchester County did elect two Liberal members.

Despite being the only female elected to the legislature at that time, I was very comfortable as a member both in the House and in the government caucus, probably due at least in part to the fact that I had already been practicing law for several years. Throughout my term, I was named to the prestigious Law Amendments Committee, which was the busiest and most demanding of the various standing committees of the House of Assembly. I was also named chair of the Standing Committee on Education which was called upon to hold public hearings concerning the potential merger of the Nova Scotia Technical College with Dalhousie University.

It was an exciting time in the late 1960s and early 1970s: the Vietnam War was finally coming to an end; the women's movement in the United States was gathering momentum; and in Canada, Pierre Elliott Trudeau had been elected prime minister. In 1974, the prime minister campaigned across the country for re-election with his spouse, Margaret Trudeau. His campaign included a rally at Truro in recognition of the Liberal wins in Colchester County. Change was the order of the day.

During my term, relevant issues included the call for legislation to provide for equal division of matrimonial property between spouses. The Liberal government introduced an appropriate bill which was well-received by members of the House and easily passed. Among other justice matters, the government had introduced legislation to provide for compensation to victims of crime, including 'rape,' as it was then called. However, the initial bill called for compensation in that instance only if pregnancy resulted. Of course, this was a glaring limitation, unacceptable to women. Following debate at the Law Amendments Committee, and it required debate, fellow members recognized the error, made correction, the bill was returned to the House and was approved as amended.

Following the election in 1974, there was agitation both locally and more broadly for Colchester County to again be represented at the cabinet table, not unreasonable given that for twenty years previous the constituency had been represented in cabinet by such prominent persons as Honourable R. L. Stanfield and G. I. Smith, QC, as premiers.

I do not know what the considerations were, but that did not occur. It made no material difference to me, as my initial and continuing interests were with the law as my professional career, not politics. At that time, being an MLA was for most members really an adjunct to one's primary occupation, as the stipend was $5,000 per year rising to $7,500 in 1978. The sittings of the House were limited to two sessions of approximately nine weeks, spring and fall, and there was no office support provided. Being an MLA at that time was not a full-time occupation unless appointed to a senior cabinet position.

However, I do think that it was a missed opportunity, a lost opportunity, on several fronts, that a member representing Colchester County was not appointed to cabinet at that time. More perhaps could have been accomplished not only then but in subsequent years as well. When the announcement was made that I would not reoffer, the *Halifax Herald* commented that the province had lost an effective, pragmatic politician.

In more recent years, there have been some remarkable women who have taken their seats in the provincial House of Assembly, including: the leader of the New Democratic Party, Alexa McDonough in the 1980s; Diane Brushett, elected as a Liberal for the federal constituency of Cumberland-Colchester; Eleanor Norrie in the 1990s for the Liberal Party in Truro-Bible Hill, who was appointed to cabinet; and Lenore Zann, again for Truro-Bible Hill, in the 2000s for the New Democratic Party, to name just a few. However, it was not easy through earlier years for women to gain nomination in a winnable seat. It was also difficult for women to aspire to political office without financial independence and firm support systems which often required putting family life, so to speak, on the back burner, particularly where young children were involved.

And, of course, politics is a very competitive undertaking, indeed rough at times, not one that necessarily appeals to many women. But those to whom it does appeal are entitled to be there. Today much has changed. Women are well-positioned to take their proper places in the political life of this province and country. They are well-educated, well-employed across society, have greater financial and personal independence and are now recognized as leaders in their communities. Family life is a shared responsibility. Some considerations: first, they must choose to be there, to enter the fray. Second, they must have their support systems in place. Not a great deal more has to be changed at this point for women to win election in greater numbers and those who win elections do very well. However, it will also require determination, qualification, and some good luck!

We can and should aspire to electing women to office at all levels including to the highest political offices our democracy offers, both as prime minister and as provincial premiers. It could be said that Nova Scotia has been somewhat narrow in this matter, but that too can change.

Certainly, my election to the Nova Scotia Legislature in 1974 by the people of Colchester County, coming so unexpectedly as it did, was a great honour and privilege, a singular experience. I thoroughly enjoyed—relished—the opportunity to be an advocate, and a strong advocate, it was said, representing the interests and the people of my constituency. However, with law having been my chosen career, in 1976 I left Nova Scotia Legal Aid to open an independent office for the practice of law in Truro. I consider myself very fortunate indeed to have had a good practice and a good life in Colchester County for more than forty years. I can recommend elected politics to aspiring women, as both elected politics and the practice of law have been most satisfying and very rewarding experiences for me.

Alexa McDonough sitting in her chair from the House of Commons

3. ALEXA MCDONOUGH, OC, ONS
NDP MLA FOR HALIFAX CHEBUCTO 1981–1993; NDP MLA FOR HALIFAX FAIRVIEW 1993–1995
Leader NSNDP 1980
First woman in Canada to lead a major recognized political party
MP for Halifax 1997–2008
Leader of Canada's New Democrats 1995-2003

I grew up in a family that was very politically oriented. My grandfather was a big activist, very much on the progressive end of politics. My father ran for office four times and never got elected. I was actually born in Ottawa, because my father was working for the Co-operative Commonwealth Federation (CCF).[5] My mother was also always very interested [in politics], and she was president of the women's organization that existed within the CCF. She influenced me to realize that politics is not just the domain of men. They both strived to open my eyes to the big, wide world out there. And they did.

> **For me, it was never a question of '*will I go into politics?*' or '*can I be in politics if there are no women there?*'—it was just a question of how many of us women we were going to be able to get there.**

---

[5] The CCF is the predecessor to the current New Democratic Party of Canada.

My educational background and early career path was in social work. Social work was a match with many of my ideals at the time. I worked at the city of Halifax in Social Planning and taught at the Maritime School of Social Work. In those same years, I started a family and became the proud mother of two boys, Justin and Travis. Politically, I first ran in the 1979 federal election, and again in 1980 with no hope of getting elected. It is not a loss if you do not get elected. It is not a loss to put your name forward and talk about and advance the many issues.

I did get elected to the Nova Scotia Legislature (MLA, Halifax Chebucto, later known as Halifax Fairview) in 1981. By then, I was the Leader of the NSNDP, a position I held until 1994. In 1995, I was elected leader of the federal New Democratic Party and won a seat in the House of Commons in 1997. Just as it was on the provincial level as MLA, it was an even greater honour to serve in public office as Halifax MP until I resigned from politics altogether in 2008. I returned to academia as Interim President of Mount Saint Vincent University in 2009.

One of the things that has become somewhat infamous from my time as an MLA was the fact that I fought for a women's washroom [in the legislature]. Those were just the things you had to do back then. Frankly, there was nothing particularly dramatic about any of the battles we fought. We did it because it had to be done. In fact, waiting in a line-up at the public washroom downstairs at the legislature enabled me to speak to many women about their daily lives, what was important to them, and how to advance those issues with them.

Slowly but persistently, the NDP started to knock down barriers and more women were elected. We founded new organizations, one federally and one provincially, one called the Participation of Women (POW) and the other called the Women in the Legislature (WIL) fund. I was very involved in the POW committee and was always involved in organizing and recruiting candidates. I was hell-bent that we needed equity in both of our governing Houses.

I always said that change will occur for women when there is a strong, progressive *left* movement. In that way, it was always about more than just getting women involved, and building a progressive movement was important to me. I loved being in politics. We took on a host of political issues over the years, often referred to as 'women's issues'—pay equity, human rights, child care, education, reproductive rights, racial discrimination, justice—feminism. My lens was always oriented to be focused that way.

A favourite aunt of mine, Peggy Shaw, who had a stellar career herself in New York theatre and retired to Halifax, knew me well and she knew about that lens. She used to come to the Nova Scotia Legislature sittings almost every day and I would get a little memo from the pages saying, "I'm up here." I'd look up and Aunt Peggy would be up in the gallery. She would be in the gallery, digesting every issue and later talking about them, and always asking endless questions. Aunt Peggy politicized more young women than I could count. She would talk to young women and say, "You've never been to the Legislature? Do it! Go over there and see Lexie!" Her heartfelt enthusiasm for the political process was an inspiration to me.

Whatever or whomever we are inspired by, I encourage anyone to run for public office. Even if you run in seats that were once thought not to be 'winnable.' That is yesterday's thinking. It is a win to be in the race. It is a win to be putting your voice, your knowledge, skills, and abilities forward.

I have attempted, through political office, to influence the way some things have gone over the years. With varying degrees of success, but always giving it my best shot. And often making noise about the issues I was working on. I often think of the words of Nellie McClung, social activist and politician, who was instrumental in Manitoba being the first province in Canada in 1916 to give women the right to vote *and* run for political office.

'Disturbers are never popular—nobody ever really loved an alarm clock in action—no matter how grateful they may have been afterward for its kind services!' — Nellie McClung, *In Times Like These*

Photo courtesy of Nova Scotia Legislature

4. The HONOURABLE MAXINE COCHRAN (1926 – 2014)
PC MLA FOR LUNENBURG CENTRE 1984–1988
First female Cabinet Minister
Minister responsible for the Advisory Council on the Status of Women
Minister of Transportation
Minister of Consumer Affairs
Minister of Culture, Recreation and Fitness

This excerpt is written by Maxine's Son, Andrew Cochran.

Outside was clear and sunny, the last day of February 1985. Inside, the Honourable Alan R. Abraham, the lieutenant governor, had read the Speech from the Throne, opening the first session of the fifty-fourth General Assembly of Nova Scotia. My mother was on her feet, her first time speaking in the House, moving the Address in Reply to the speech. First, the pleasantries of the day: thanking His Honour, noting the wisdom of re-electing the Speaker, congratulating the Leader of the Opposition for his first session in that office. Special congratulations went to the premier for becoming one of only five in the province's history elected for a third term. She waited for the sustained applause to subside, then noted the death of a former House member. It marked the end of the beginning of her speech.

She paused. Above and to her right, the wives of the members looked on from the gallery. She continued, "Mr. Speaker…for ten years on opening day I sat in your gallery, the Speaker's Gallery, and I want to pay tribute to the women sitting there this afternoon and to the contribution they are making to public life in this province."

My father had been the member for Lunenburg Centre for ten years, and they always attended openings together. Now, my mother was the first woman to succeed her husband in the same seat in the House of Assembly. A few months later she would become the first female cabinet minister in the province. Naturally, that is how she is most remembered. But it was her journey from the gallery to the floor, and before, that defined her approach to politics.

She was an early believer in women having engaging careers no matter where they were. It could be outside the home or inside. What mattered more to her was the participation, being part of something bigger, contributing the value of a woman's point of view.

She earned a Bachelor of Science in Home Economics from Acadia University after growing up in Lawrencetown, Annapolis County, the older of two girls. Her early career was with the Canadian Red Cross, as director of homemaker services in Nova Scotia. When she married my father in 1951, they sold their possessions and went on an extended honeymoon in Europe. The trip lasted several months. The romance lasted until my father died—a heart attack, suddenly, aboard a train in my mother's arms, 33 years later. She was devastated.

One evening, some months later, the premier [John Buchanan] came for a visit. He wanted to see how she was doing. My father's seat, Lunenburg Centre, was still vacant. There needed to be a by-election. Might she be interested in running? It was a politically astute move for a political party wanting to retain a seat. But it made objective sense, too.

As well as being side-by-side with my father during his three successful elections and subsequent public duties as a cabinet member, my mother had a considerable resume. In the early 1960s she was a host/interviewer on CBC Television in Halifax, doing programs and segments about issues for women and family life. Then she taught home economics at Queen Elizabeth High School in Halifax. After that she became the first director of public relations for the IWK Children's Hospital, helping plan the opening of the new hospital in 1970.

As a community volunteer, she had been a founding member of the Vanier Institute of the Family, national president of the Canadian Home Economics Association, national board member of the Association of Canadian Radio and Television Artists, president of the Junior League of Halifax, vice-president of the Halifax-Dartmouth Welfare Council, and board member of the Maritime School of Social Work.

She stood for the nomination, was selected, ran, and won the by-election. A friend delivered a framed line-drawing of the House of Assembly exterior with the caption, 'a woman's place is in the House.' Five months later, she campaigned again in the provincial general election and won.

By the time she stood to give the Address in Reply, she had been life-partner in three successive elections and a candidate in two, about which she said, "…although I would certainly not have chosen the circumstances that brought about my election, I am nevertheless proud to succeed my late husband in representing the great constituency of Lunenburg Centre and the people who stood so solidly behind me on two occasions last year."

The honour that created her public legacy came later that year. In November 1985, she was sworn in as a member of cabinet, the first woman cabinet minister in Nova Scotia, and, she liked to say, the first woman to succeed her husband in the executive council. It wasn't a statement of competitiveness but of closeness, as if a seat at the cabinet table gave her a richer memory of their life together.

But that was when she had time for reflective moments. Her first portfolio was the Department of Transportation, among the largest and most costly for the province and its 26,000 kilometres of roads and highways. She saw it as a connector of people, their goods, services, families, and friends. She attacked learning the ways and means of the department as she did any task: curiosity for the facts, regard for the experts, a focus on the people impacted, a desire to know how adversities could be made better. We would drive back and forth between Mahone Bay and the city and soon she was providing a running commentary of every overpass, change in road surface, construction zone, highway sign placement, etc. She had become fascinated by it all. The continuing theme was road safety and what could be done.

Learning new things was her approach to life. It would go on being applied as she took on responsibilities as Minister of Consumer Affairs, Minister of Culture, Recreation, and Fitness, Minister responsible for the Residential Tenancies Act, Minister responsible for the Heritage Property Act, and Minister responsible for the Advisory Council on the Status of Women.

Meanwhile, 1986 held another first. The House heard from the member for Cumberland Centre, a member of the opposition, rising in a gesture of camaraderie: "Mr. Speaker, I would like to draw to your attention, and to the attention of all members of this House, that we have in our midst today, a grandmother for the first time, the Minister of Transportation."

A little more than two years later, she weighed a decision that was similar to one she had already faced. There was another election coming in the fall of 1988. Would she run? By now, she knew and loved constituency work. She knew and loved the opportunity to encourage young people, especially young women, to get involved in politics. She knew, and loved, the fact that there were three women sitting in the legislative assembly. She told the House, "Nova Scotians in both urban and rural constituencies have signalled clearly their willingness to elect women to this House, to elect candidates on the basis of their record, their ability and their support of, or opposition to, the government, regardless of their sex."

From the election of Gladys Porter, the first woman in the House, until now, had taken a generation. Perhaps it was another end of another beginning.

She knew she still had more to learn, and perhaps still the time. Her final decision about what to do next, she said, was obvious. She wanted to learn more about being a grandmother.

Photo courtesy of Dr. Tom Urbaniak

5. CORA ETTER (1924 – 2020)
PC MLA FOR HANTS EAST 1984–1988
Councillor for Municipality of East Hants

Written by Dr. Tom Urbaniak. Dr. Tom Urbaniak is married to Cora's granddaughter Rev. Alison Etter. Tom is a professor of political science at Cape Breton University. This article is adapted from his "Political Insights" column of November 6, 2019, which appeared in the **Cape Breton Post** *and affiliated newspapers.*

The conservatism of Cora Etter was and is progressive.

Her dignified, empathetic, practical style of leadership is a lesson to today's national Conservative Party as it does some much-needed soul searching. As a teacher, pharmacy proprietor and businessperson in Shubenacadie, Hants County, Cora was drawn into politics by her neighbours. She was seen as a trusted, smart organizer who could solve problems without a fuss.

Cora moved Robert Stanfield's nomination for Tory candidate in his constituency in 1956, the same year that Stanfield became premier. In 1960, Cora ran successfully for the municipal council of East Hants after becoming concerned about conditions in a municipal home for people with disabilities.

She was one of Nova Scotia's trailblazing women municipal politicians. Cora would serve on the council for two decades, taking charge of many projects and committees. She was nicknamed 'the mayor of Shubenacadie.'

In 1984, Cora was elected to the Nova Scotia House of Assembly. She was one of just three women in the legislature and only the fifth woman ever to be elected. In her first speech in the House, Cora shed light on her philosophy: "Mr. Speaker, we cannot survive in watertight compartments."

She supported free enterprise but argued that business "must scrupulously observe the obligation" that comes with freedom. And that obligation is to community: "I believe it is sometimes hard to separate the corporation from the community, because more often than not they are one and the same thing. At least this is so in East Hants, for people who work in business are drawn from the community that surrounds it…and they must be mindful of their social responsibilities to the community."

This is certainly not an ideology of rugged individualism or maximization of corporate profits.

It was Cora's organic conservatism that led her to champion pay equity for women—the right to equal pay for work of equal value. When the PC government finally introduced legislation in 1988, Cora stood in the House and said: "Hallelujah."

She was 'disturbed' by chamber of commerce spokespeople who claimed that the concept of pay equity would somehow hurt the economy. "Most importantly…pay equity for women will mean a better standard of living for them and their families." But Cora cautioned that the work of pursuing equality is not done. "Also, we must improve education and training, better child care facilities and so forth. It is a goal we must work toward as we step into the 1990s."

This vision of society as a rooted, compassionate community of free citizens came through again when Cora, as a member of the governing party, endorsed an opposition motion on home care for seniors: "I see older people as just not a group set aside. I think they are an integral part of our life."

In one of her final speeches in the House, Cora supported progressive environmental assessment legislation. She invoked the interesting argument that it would cut through red tape and bureaucracy by giving communities a more direct role to scrutinize development proposals for themselves.

In reviewing Hansard, the author of this profile could not find one instance of Cora insulting or mocking another politician or party. Her remarks were calm and structured. Her interventions contained relevant facts and were filled with tangible examples from her Hants East constituency.

"No, I cannot altogether agree with that." That's how she reflectively started a fulsome response to a question posed to her in the assembly by NDP leader Alexa McDonough.

Cora lost her seat in the 1988 election to Liberal Jack Hawkins. But she remained active in business and in her community. In 1993, she received the Canadian Women in Business Lifetime Achievement Award. The citation noted, among other things, Cora's mentorship of young women in business and politics.

Part of the recent family lore is a letter Cora sent to Stephen Harper when he was prime minister. She was not happy with many aspects of his approach and direction. Apparently, Cora had second thoughts after she put that letter in the mailbox. She was a team player after all. But she is also a thinker, a dedicated leader and a pioneer in many ways. And she has served Nova Scotia very well.

6. The HONOURABLE SANDY JOLLY
LIBERAL MLA FOR DARTMOUTH NORTH 1988-1998
Minister of Municipal Affairs
Minister of Business and Consumer Services

I was born and raised in Kentville, and attended school there. I went to Mount Saint Vincent University and graduated in 1975 with a business degree. When I graduated, I went into the life insurance industry, of which there were very few women at the time, particularly right out of university. I was the first female employee benefit consultant at Mutual Life of Canada, so I had to go through quite an interview process to get this job. I started my own company, Young Jolly Agencies, with a partner in 1984. I worked in the company for five years, until I was elected. I also did a lot of volunteer work and I became the chairperson of the board for Victorian Order of Nurses, and chairperson for the board for Adsum House.

The riding of Dartmouth North conducted a survey which said if they could find a strong woman candidate, then the Liberals would have a chance of winning the riding. It was held by the Reverent Laird Sterling at the time. My name came up through various people. I didn't have a membership in any political party at the time.

The Dartmouth North President Don Valardo invited me to come for a breakfast meeting and asked if I would be interested in being the candidate for Dartmouth North. I was still only four years into having my own business, and I said, "No. I know nothing about politics." That weekend, I went to Cape

Breton to visit my younger sister who is married to a man from West Bay. I told him the story about being asked, and my brother-in-law said, "What's the downside if you said yes? If you run and you win and [the Liberals] win government, you'll be either one of or the only women who's going to be in a government. Two, if you run and you win, and the Liberals don't become government, you'll still have a high profile. Three, if you run and you don't win, your name and your picture will be all over Dartmouth. When you go making business calls they will say, 'oh yeah, I know who you are.' I don't see what the downside is."

I came back after that weekend on Monday and I called Mr. Valardo and said, "If you're still interested and if you haven't found anyone else, I would be interested in talking further."

Once I was elected in 1988, I became the finance critic and deputy house leader. Out of the twenty-one [Liberal] members, nineteen were men and two were women—it was only Eleanor Norrie and I. Vince MacLean eventually stepped down as leader, and we had a leadership contest. I supported Dr. Savage, and he won. We had an election in 1993 and became government. I became the Minister of Municipal Affairs and a number of other boards.

Under that government, after much discussion, we decided that we needed to amalgamate some of the municipalities in Nova Scotia. We first did the four metropolitan municipalities: Halifax, Dartmouth, Bedford, and Halifax County. Next, eight municipalities in Cape Breton. Nobody was happy about it, though now they say it is working well. I was the Minister responsible for overseeing these amalgamations.

I did not find that I faced sexism within my party. There might have been a couple of old school guys that were around when we were in opposition who just were not used to having women in politics. Vince MacLean and Dr. John Savage were both men who did not believe in that old school way of thinking.

I was fortunate enough to enjoy the work I did all the way through. I enjoyed being in the insurance industry and I enjoyed being in politics, both of which were male-dominated fields. I think one of the interesting things about my story is that I had no desire or ambition to be in politics. It was something that just happened. I'm very happy that I did it. It's a very unusual opportunity and I think if someone gets that opportunity, they should take it.

The advice I would give is that you have to stay true to yourself. The one thing that I was able to do was look in the mirror and say, "Okay, I'm comfortable with myself, what I'm doing and how I'm doing it."

You also cannot be super sensitive, and that's one of the difficulties we run into today. You can't let somebody walk all over you but at the same time, you can't be battling people all the time.

The thing I was most happy about was the opportunity to help people in the constituency. You were able to give them a voice, especially in social assistance. So many people were on social assistance or were single parents. Life was really tough. If I could call somebody on their behalf, I would. If there's anything I'm proud of, it was to be able to be a voice for people. To have a better understanding of what they were going through. But by the grace of God, a lot of us would be going through those things if we were born into a different family, had educational difficulties, or had problems with mental or physical health. Some people just needed a voice. They needed somebody to stand up for them. It was an opportunity to be a voice for people, and that was really important.

Photo courtesy of Marie Dechman

7. The HONOURABLE MARIE DECHMAN
PC MLA FOR LUNENBURG WEST 1988-1993
First female Deputy Speaker
Minister of Community Services
Minister of Consumer Affairs and Minister responsible for Housing

I've always been involved politically and interested in politics. I served on the executive of both federal and provincial ridings in the South Shore of Nova Scotia for many years. That piqued my interest in running for office, and I thought that maybe I could contribute something to the province. There were very few women in the legislature at the time—Alexa McDonough was actually the only one for quite a while. I discussed the idea of running with some friends of mine, and they said, "go for it." That's how it all happened—it was based on my experience after years of being involved with the party.

When I wanted to put my name forward, there was already someone running for the Progressive Conservatives—Harry Cook, who had been the mayor of Bridgewater for many years. He was running for the seat as a Conservative, but his history was Liberal. We had a convention, the largest convention that had ever been held for the Lunenburg West constituency. It was packed, with standing room only. There was one other man running. I won on the second ballot.

I think the most important point for me as a member, and a woman, is that I had a long history of working in the party before running. I knew every member in the Conservative party, and by acquaintance some members of the other parties. When I was elected, I was not a stranger. I walked into a caucus full of forty-two men as the only woman, but I didn't feel uncomfortable at all, and that was due to my previous involvement in the party. I am a businesswoman and voiced my opinion without any intimidation. There were pretty strong, powerful men in that caucus, but I felt welcomed and respected.

I was the first female deputy Speaker in Nova Scotia. The first time I sat was the first instance of a woman being in that role. A woman had never presided over the legislature before—ever. Never sat in that chair. It was a big challenge. But the members of every party were highly respectful. I tried, in turn, to do the same to them—to pay attention to what they were saying. As a speaker it can be very boring, you sit for hours and hours and listen to every person's opinion. But they appreciated that I listened, and it made me learn even more by really hearing what everyone had to say.

I was also the Minister of Community Services. It was a huge portfolio. I took at least three hours of every day and studied as much as I could about every facet of that department. It was a fascinating challenge. I was quite shocked by some of the things that I learned in that role, especially as a woman. There were so many programs and facilities at the time for men with addictions or problems, but very little for women. There was a gap in services for women between the ages of sixty and sixty-five. If they became homeless, there was nothing for them. We still have not come to the point where we have fully addressed this problem.

As a fiscal conservative, I was concerned about finances and the economic stability of the province… but not at the expense of helping people who were living in poverty or having problems. One of the pieces of legislation I brought forth as minister covered payment for pharmaceutical items for the children of parents who were on welfare. When I was first elected, parents were covered under the legislation for their drugs, but their children were not. If you have a mother living in a poverty situation, say with three children, and she would go to the doctor with one of her children with an earache—and the doctor was covered, but the prescription could not be filled if she didn't have the money. Pain and sickness in a poor child is the same as in a child who happens to have money. I presented that change. The truth is, it wasn't a favourable change with everyone. Premier Donald Cameron only asked me one question— "Did you research everything and is it the right thing to do?" When I told him that it was, he agreed. He trusted me as a minister. He was a very good premier, underestimated by many people. He put a lot of faith in his ministers.

I think I represented women who were struggling with life. I tried to do as much as I possibly could in terms of accommodation and safe homes for women. The pharmacare program was a turning point for many children who lived in a poverty situation. That was the best thing that I could have done. I also intervened in situations to challenge the legislation regarding the way nursing homes were run, and the way private senior residences operated. Those were all aspects of my portfolio.

I might sound like a Liberal, not a Conservative. Many people think Conservatives are only interested in the fiscal of running the government, the business aspect of it and the economy. They think we are not oriented towards the social aspects of life. I have to say, that is not true. It is a misconception. That stigma is still attached to the party, and we have to overcome that. Most Conservatives do believe people should have choice in their lives. Only a small minority would say otherwise. All of the members I ever knew over the years had as much concern for those issues as any other party. Alexa McDonough and I were good friends. She was with the NDP party, who is known as the party of social justice. I was a little more cautious with policy than she was, but we both believed in the same goal.

One thing people should know about this job is that it is very demanding. If you are a young mother, it might be very difficult. There are still barriers there if you cannot afford to have nannies or daycare. If you become a minister, your demands to travel are enormous. It is a big move for young women with a family, and that is still a barrier to women's participation.

I would encourage young women to become active and study. If you want to be good at something, you must study and participate. Anyone who thinks they can be a member of a parliament of any kind and not spend hours studying and learning is wrong. When I was elected, I became deputy Speaker, and I studied sixteen hours a day for weeks before the legislature opened.

It was a tremendous honour to serve and be an elected member. I always thought that I tried to put my constituency first. It's not always possible, as it is a balancing act; but one is never successful in being re-elected if they don't pay close attention to their constituency.

8. The HONOURABLE FRANCENE COSMAN
LIBERAL MLA FOR BEDFORD-FALL RIVER 1993–1999
Minister of Community Services
Minister responsible for the Advisory Council on the Status of Women
Minister of Human Resources
Deputy Speaker
Mayor of Bedford 1979–1982
Councillor for Halifax County 1976–1979

Formally, my education is in nursing. I completed a three-year diploma program and a post-graduate diploma in nursing. I have always had an issues-oriented personality. If there was an important issue, I always got involved. I guess I would say I was an activist. I was writing letters to the newspapers at the age of sixteen, so I have always paid attention to what's going on around me. Being in nursing, I started looking at things going on in my own backyard.

    I was asked to run for the seat as [Bedford] district councilor, and I won that. There were a lot of planning issues in Bedford that people were not happy with. As a district, Bedford was not being listened to by the local government. We went to the Public Utilities Board and asked to become a town. Ultimately the board decided we could become a town and I had been highly active in that fight. It was a huge accomplishment—setting up a new town from scratch is no easy deal. People were coming to me and saying, "You've done a lot of work, why don't you run to be the first mayor?" I thought about it, and thought, *why not*? I did run against two others—two men, and I beat them handily. That was fun.

I served one term [as mayor of Bedford], and then the provincial government asked me to become the president of the Advisory Council of the Status of Women. After four years in that role, I did not think the government was listening to us on issues that were important, so I quit. I had my own protest movement. I went to work as the executive director of the Liberal Party, partly because I was mad at the Tories for not doing enough for women. I worked with them for four years, and then I ran as an MLA in 1993. I won under the government of Premier John Savage.

I am a feminist, I've been a feminist since as long as I can remember, and I'm pro-choice. At my nomination meeting, there was a lot of buzz going on that I was 'pro-abortion.' I knew something was cooking and I thought I was going to lose the nomination. I had a nice little speech I was going to make, and I just took my speech and ripped it up. I stood up at the podium and I said, "There's a buzz in the room about abortion rights. I want you to hear my position on it and then you can judge me, once you know exactly how I think."

I explained to them that as a nurse, I had many patients who had botched abortions and died. Because there was no such thing as a legal abortion in the 1960s, I saw illegal abortions happen. I explained that I had two teenage daughters, and if they happened to get pregnant and came to me, I would sit down with them and tell them all the options that were available for them. But if their decision in the end was to have an abortion, I would support them. I said that, right there, with 1,500 people in the room. The buzz all died down, and I got nominated. It pays to speak your truth.

[Premier Savage] decided, along with his cabinet, that all the urban area and out into the county was going to be amalgamated as the Halifax Regional Municipality. That caused quite a ruckus for Bedford, because we had only been a town since 1980. The premier, and my party, was going to tear that all apart when it was something I had fought for. In truth, Bedford could not stand on its own with Halifax, Dartmouth, and the rest of the county surrounding us. We would be this little sixty square kilometre block, and we were still contracting out a lot of services. It put us between a rock and a hard place. Our government went ahead with amalgamation. I did a lot of fighting behind the scenes. I was happy to be on the inside of the tent engaging in the battle, rather than outside the tent looking in. It was a very, very troublesome time for me as an MLA. Many people in my riding were upset about the amalgamation.

In that time period under Dr. John Savage, I was the party whip. I had to make sure everyone was there for the vote when the House was sitting. Later, I was put in the position of deputy Speaker. The deputy Speaker chairs the whole House when budget time is on, so it is a significant role because you must make sure everything is going along smoothly. There was a steep learning curve in that role. I had this big Speakers book that I would read when I would come home at night and think, *what am I doing in this job?*

When Russell McLellan became premier, he put me in cabinet as Minister of Community Services. In cabinet positions, there's a pecking order. It's called the 'Order of Precedence,' based on how big the department is and how big its budget is. The Finance Minister sits next to the premier, and then the Minister of Health, followed by the Minister of Community Services. The first day I went to a cabinet meeting I sat at the far end because I thought, *I'm new here, I'll take the back end of the table.* But the clerk to cabinet said, "No, it's the order of precedence you have to sit up here!"

It was the quietest things that I was able to achieve, that would never have made the *hurray for you!* moments in newspaper clippings, that make me the proudest. I had a constituent here in Bedford who had ALS. He was in the hospital for a year and a half because there was no way to treat him at home, even though he wanted to die at home and have his family with him. It was costing the government $3,000 a day to keep him in the hospital. I thought, *why don't we do a pilot project and put nursing care in the home right around the clock, letting him go home and be nursed there till he dies?*

It was less expensive. There was some resistance to doing it, but I [fought]. That was one of several times that I was able to make a significant difference quietly. Those are the things I'm proud of. The things I know I did for people behind the scenes. Most people think politics is about getting your headline, but for me it is not really about the quiet accomplishments and what you can do for your constituents.

[Being a woman] in politics was quite fascinating because I am very aware of how women are perceived. One man said to me, "I'll never vote for a skirt!" I just looked at him as though he had a hole in his head. I argued with him at the door. I literally put my foot in the door when he tried to slam it in my face. I said, "I'm not going to give up that easily."

He kept listing all of the traits that women had that made him not want to vote for one. He said, "You're a nit-picker!" I said, "No, I pay attention to detail."

He went through all these negative stereotypes, and I refuted every single one. When we were finished, he said, "I've changed my mind. I'm going to vote for you." I remember that just like it was yesterday. There were many times when people would say they would not vote for a woman, that you did not know what you were doing, and that you should stay home and raise your children—I got that a lot.

You know you are going to face similar things, that's our society. There's social conditioning for women that we aren't equal, we're sex objects, and we're not treated with the equality and respect that we're due. I think that you have to be strong to run for politics, and you can't be sensitive to other peoples' rudeness and ignorance. Just plant your feet hard on the ground, stand up, and be counted, because there will always be opposition to women moving up the ladder and getting ahead.

Photo courtesy of Tim O'Connor

9. LILA O'CONNOR (1940 – 2017)
LIBERAL MLA FOR LUNENBURG 1993–1998
Town Councillor in Mahone Bay 1988–1993/2004–2012

This excerpt is written by Lila's son, Tim O'Connor.

Lila O'Connor was the MLA for the constituency of Lunenburg after winning a very hard-fought election in a riding that, since 1953, was only once ever held by a Liberal member. After years of being an organizer and executive within the riding and on the provincial level where Lila was the first female member of the Lunenburg Centre Executive of the Liberal Party, she was ready to take a run at a riding that was only once ever held by a woman. She had campaigned in the 1988 nominations, where she lost in her attempt to win the nod to represent the Liberals, but Lila was not one to go quietly into the night. First, she worked as hard on the 1988 election as if she were the candidate herself, but the Liberals lost by 1,047 votes to the Progressive Conservative candidate. In the 1984 election, Lila was the campaign manager for the Liberal candidate.

    Lila wanted to contribute, so she ran to work within the municipal government level as a councilor in the town of Mahone Bay. Lila and her husband Michael were respected leaders within the town and were volunteers in many organizations and committees in the areas of health, welfare, and education,

She was a pillar in the establishment of the Victorian Order of Nurses branch in Lunenburg County. Her time on council was used to work hard to make Mahone Bay a jewel in the province, one where you would want to live, work, and raise a family. Lila was the mother of three and became a grandmother of nine.

Within the Liberal Party, Lila had been a delegate to several conferences, both on the provincial level and the federal level, and she also served on several committees including the Liberal Task Force on Concerns of Women and the South Shore Liberal Search Committee.

When the election of 1993 was approaching, Lila was nominated as a candidate, but was opposed, so the campaign to have Lila O'Connor the Liberal candidate for the election began. Many people joined her camp, including: Joe Feeney and his wife Barbara, Franceen Romney, Pat Burke, Billy Bruhn, Sylvia Knox. Her family, all taking active roles and fulfilling the tasks assigned by her husband Michael, who was always there, mainly in the shadows, supporting his wife. The hard work of Lila's team paid off and she was to be the candidate for the Liberal Party in the riding of Lunenburg Centre, and after the general election, Lila became the member of the legislative assembly for Lunenburg Centre, swinging over 1,300 votes from the 1988 election.

The 1993 general election brought the Liberals led by Dr. John Savage back to power, and it was Premier Savage that gave Lila the nickname of the 'Bulldog of the Caucus,' as Lila would not back down when it came to ensuring her riding was given the full attention it deserved. Both the Lunenburg West and Chester-St. Margaret's ridings also went to the Liberals, and Don Downe became the member for Lunenburg West. Don writes:

"My first opportunity to really get to know Lila was when I ran for the leadership of the Liberal Party of Nova Scotia back in 1992. She was an extraordinarily strong supporter and was instrumental in my candidacy however, our friend, the late John Savage, was victorious. Lila and I both continued our political careers by running in the next provincial election. The mark of a great leader can always be seen in the people they are able to bring to their team. Joe Feeney (former mayor of Mahone Bay), and many more worked almost as hard as Lila and her husband Michael to win the Lunenburg riding in 1993, and so her provincial political journey began. It has been said that Lila was a bit of a bulldog, but I would like to say she was tenacious, hard-working, and would never accept 'no' as an answer. As a cabinet minister I realized that when Lila needed something from one of my departments, she was going to get her way!

"Lila represented an incredibly challenging riding that included the towns of Mahone Bay and Lunenburg, plus a large rural area. Lila worked hard to ensure ongoing support for Fisherman's Memorial Hospital and to maintain both the veterans wing and the emergency department. Roads were key for everyone and Lila made sure she got her fair share of the budget. Lila took her responsibilities as an MLA and a caucus member very seriously. She was highly active within caucus promoting women's rights, transparency of government, and the importance of helping those in need. It truly was an honour to call Lila a dear friend."

While the MLA, Lila was given responsibilities with the provincial Department of Tourism, being named legislative assistant to Tourism Minister Ross Bragg. She filled in at functions for the minister, met with various groups, reported back to the minister, and presided over openings for various festivals and events. Lila had a strong understanding of the tourism industry in Nova Scotia and her experience and opinions were sought after by the cabinet.

Lila also became the chairperson of the Human Resource Committee, legislative assistant to the Minister of Economic Development, and sat on the Public Accounts, Economic Development, and Utilities Committees.

Lila's love of Canada was at full force as she marched during the massive Unity Rally in Montreal ahead of the 1995 Quebec referendum on sovereignty.

Within her constituency, Lila worked as hard as any member. She learned all the various industries within the riding including forestry (as the Christmas Tree Capital of the World was within her riding) as well fisheries (as the Fishing Capital of Canada, Lunenburg was within her riding). As well, her riding may have had more miles of road than any other riding, so the always controversial road up-keep strategy was constantly being scrutinized. Lila travelled them extensively, going to every community event she could, often with some of her grandchildren in tow as she never neglected family during her time as a member. Her grandchildren were proud of her and she has much to do with them becoming the strong individuals that they have become today. They all became accustomed to answering the phone at 'Grammie's' house and tell whoever was calling that, "Lila wasn't home, she was at a meeting!"

Lila passed away on December 5, 2017, and her husband Michael passed away June 21, 2019. They are both missed greatly by their family and friends, and also by the people they crossed paths with throughout their lives, and their children and grandchildren are reminded of this each time they cross paths with one of these people.

In Lila's own words, here is a passage from her last speech given as a politician. She writes:

"I was born in Washington, D.C. on March 11, 1940, to Lucy and Allan Burnett and adopted by my grandparents, John and Vivian Macdonald. After living in various parts of Canada we settled in Bridgewater and enjoyed some of my happiest years with classmates and chief boyfriend Michael. Circumstances required moving back to the United States in the late 1950s, where I completed my education. Happily, in 1961, following a seven-year courtship and engagement, Michael and I were married and moved to Mahone Bay to raise our family and participate in community life with many friends. Nothing gives me more satisfaction than seeing my family, friends, and country flourish. Thank you all, Lila."

10. The HONOURABLE ELEANOR NORRIE
LIBERAL MLA FOR TRURO-BIBLE HILL 1993–1998
Minister of Civil Service (later Human Resources)
Minister of Housing and Consumer Affairs and Natural Resources

Never in my wildest dreams did I ever think I would run for any office, let alone political office. Before I was married, I was a teacher. Once I started having a family, I was a stay-at-home mom—but I stayed very involved in the community. It was more of a surprise to me than anybody that I ended up running for MLA and winning. I was very involved in the community. I had three daughters, and I was very involved in their activities, as well as my own. It seemed that wherever I was involved, I would end up in a leadership position. I was a Brownie Leader. I was the coordinator of the school band; I was the manager and president of the swim team. I belonged to the Truro Attic Painters and I ended up being the president. On the Truro Sports Heritage Society, I ended up being the chair. I guess it was either because I had a lot to say or I was willing to do a lot of work. I was always very energetic and interested in improving things.

My mother-in-law, Margaret Norrie, was very active in politics. She was one of the first women to run in Nova Scotia. She did not win, but she ran for MLA in the 1950s. She stayed very interested both locally as well as provincially, and ended up more involved federally. She was very supportive of several federal candidates and she was the president of the Liberal Women in the province. My mother was very active in politics, so I just sort of stayed true to form and was always interested in politics. My mother-in-law eventually became a senator, so that gave me an inside look on what it was like to be involved at a higher level of government, building on being one that knocked on doors and handing out pamphlets. I saw the difference you could make in an elected or appointed position.

There was a very active Liberal association in Truro-Bible Hill in the '90s. A very high-profile gentlemen within that association approached me when the 1993 election was coming up and said, "Eleanor, I think you should run." It had never even crossed my mind. I talked to my family, I talked to my husband. I thought, *Oh I'll never win, but it would be fun to try!* The timing was perfect for me. My children were all out of university and my husband was semi-retired. From a party point of view, the Liberals were well positioned to win in 1993. There was some upheaval in the local Progressive Conservative party after twenty-five years in power, so the Liberals had a real opportunity to win in Truro if they had the right candidate, the right program and right policies. I was there at the right time.

My experience as a woman in politics was very interesting. In 1993, there had been very few women elected in the legislature. Alexa McDonough was the leader of the NDP at that time. There had been one other woman elected in Truro-Bible Hill in the '70s, Melinda MacLean. She was the first woman to be elected from this area—one of the first ever. There had been very few women involved when I got there. Being a woman in politics in the '90s came with a lot of stumbling blocks. There was still this feeling that women did not quite belong there…that you had to prove yourself.

I was elected in May, and by June I was in cabinet. I had never been in politics before—I had never even run in an election before I won. There were four Liberal women elected, two of us were put in cabinet. There were many occasions that I encountered where people were either surprised that the minister was a woman, or did not want to talk to the minister if she was a woman.

I had several portfolios during my time as MLA and minister, my main one at the time was the Civil Service Commission, which included Sport and Recreation. I remember being in the House of Assembly, and question period was just finishing up. I had to be over at the Mayflower Curling Club to open the tankard for Nova Scotia. I had arranged for my daughter to pick me up and whisk me over there. She took me over and pulled in where there was a parking place. I started to get out and the parking attendant came over and said, "You can't park there! That's for the minister!" Never in his wildest dreams did he expect a woman to get out of the car. I said, "I am the minister!" If it had been a man to get out the car in a suit, he would have automatically thought they were the minister. My daughter was just shocked.

There were a lot of times where being a woman worked to my advantage. When people were not expecting a lot from you, you could overreach their expectations. I enjoyed proving people wrong. But I did feel in the House that opposition members did not respect the women ministers as much as they would men, or treat them with the same respect. There were times in the House that there was an underlying insult because you were a woman, and they would question you differently.

I think that women can make a big difference because they approach life so differently than men. I like what Justin Trudeau did with putting an equal balance in his cabinet, but I would like to turn that around and say, "Just have as many men as you do women, not just as many women as you have men." We still approach it as having men in cabinet being the default, and I think we need to start looking at it in a different way.

I am still shocked that I managed to be nominated, I managed to win, and I managed to become a cabinet minister. I was only there one term, 1993–1998, because of the history of the John Savage government. We call that government a 'difficult time,' but I think it was the best time to be in government, because you really had the opportunity to make changes. We did things differently. If we had gone down the path of the previous governments had gone, Nova Scotia would have been bankrupt.

It was a tough time in '93, '94, '95, trying to balance a budget and re-engineer government. We probably did too much, too soon, too fast. You hear now more and more people giving accolades to Dr. John Savage. I was really disappointed when he stepped down. I thought, *go for it! Run one more time*! But he could not do it to his family, so he didn't. I think people might have been pleasantly surprised what would have happened if he had stayed and run in one more election.

Since I was in government, one of the most productive things I have done is be involved in the Colchester Community Workshops. The Workshops is a facility that hires, or has clients, who are mentally challenged adults. They were working out of an older, hole-in-the-wall building on Prince Street. People did not even know that they were there. They were not given the respect or attention that they deserved. The man that was in charge of the Workshop came to about twenty of us and asked us if we would create a foundation to provide a new facility for the clients at the Workshop. Once again, I was named chair of the foundation. I was very proud to do so.

We raised the largest amount of money that any campaign had ever raised in a capital campaign in the community. Not only did we raise the $2.5 million, but we built the building. We hired the designer and we designed it. I am very proud of what we accomplished. Those clients just changed overnight. They discovered they mattered. They discovered people cared. One girl who could hardly speak to people is now in charge in the New-to-You shop—she was the cashier, and she just blossomed. Now I have a whole new group of friends. It opened in 2005 and even now, when I bump into them around town, I get a big hug.

What I am really proud of in life is my children. I have a grandson that I am really proud of. We did not have any boys, so our only grandchild is our first little boy– he is fifteen now. I'm really quite proud of him. I am also very proud of my family. We have contributed a lot in the community.

I would like to say that if the opportunity to run for office ever arose for anyone, go for it. It does not matter what party. It does not matter what your background is. If the opportunity is there, I would say go for the nomination. Work hard. Decide what you want to accomplish and just go down that path. Do not take no for an answer. I think it is an amazing profession, where you have the potential to really make an impact. It is a difficult job, but I am proud of the work that we did while I was there. I miss it. I do miss it.

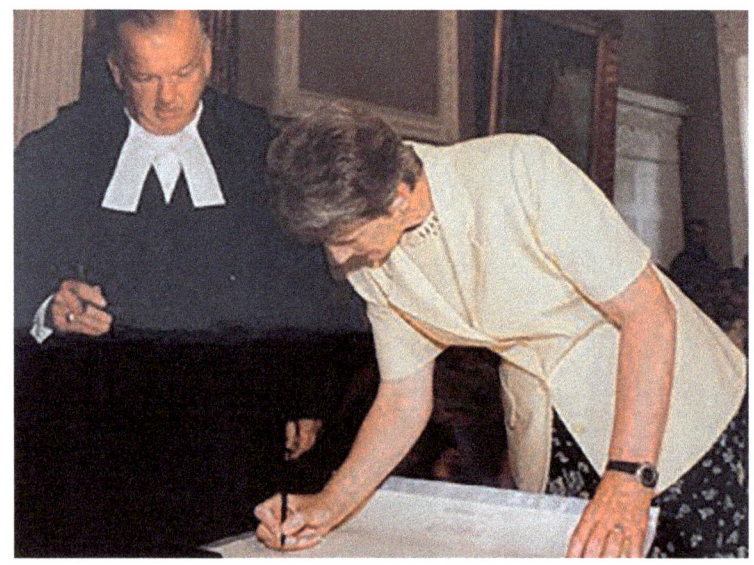 

Photos courtesy of Carolyn Carpan

11. EILEEN O'CONNELL (1947 – 2000)
NDP MLA FOR HALIFAX FAIRVIEW 1996–2000

This excerpt was written by Eileen's daughter, Carolyn Carpan. She is an academic librarian at the University of Alberta Library, and, like her mother, a writer.

When my mother, Eileen O'Connell, was diagnosed with terminal breast cancer in 1998, I asked her if there was a place she'd always wanted to go, landmarks she wanted to see, or someone she wanted to meet before she died. "I just want to do my job," she responded. After working as an English teacher in the Halifax school system for eighteen years, my mother had finally been elected in 1996 to the job she really wanted: member of the Nova Scotia House of Assembly for the New Democratic Party.

My mother wanted to play a role in the political life of Nova Scotia, where she had lived most of her life, and she wanted to help make the lives of Nova Scotians better. My mother ran and lost in provincial elections in 1984, 1998, and 1993, for seats in Halifax Citadel and Halifax Chebucto. After three losses, she gave up the idea of being an elected politician, but when her friend and mentor Alexa McDonough became the federal New Democratic Party leader in 1995, my mother's family, friends, and supporters convinced her to run for the provincial seat in Halifax Fairview. She won the seat and held it in elections in 1998 and 1999.

My mother became interested in politics at an early age. She often told the story of the time she ran for class president when she was in school and lost by one vote because she voted for her male competitor because she thought that's what you were supposed to do. The moral I took from this story was that women need to believe in themselves and vote for themselves if they are running for political office. If you don't believe in yourself, who else will?

By the time Mom was elected, there were a lot of people who believed in her political dream besides Alexa [McDonough], including her mother Jean O'Connell, her siblings Colleen, Michael, Peggy, Dan, Mary, and Caroline O'Connell, her sister-in-law and campaign manager Mary Jane White, constituency assistants Linda Smith and Alexandra Rahr, and too many friends, colleagues, and supporters in Halifax to name.

My mother taught me that everyone, no matter who they are or where they come from, deserves to be treated with respect and dignity. She cared about people and people knew they mattered to her. When friends and family needed help, she was the first one to offer a pot of tea, a meal, a bed, or help solving a problem. Her care and genuine interest in improving people's lives made her a unique politician who made friends everywhere she went, including the legislature, regardless of political party affiliation.

She continued to serve her constituents during her illness, speaking in the Nova Scotia Legislature about the hidden costs of being sick with cancer. She argued that the need for wigs is a women's issue: "Social and cultural conditions make baldness less acceptable for women than for men. Does the minister support a government policy which impacts most forcefully on poor women?" (Hansard, Assembly 57, Session 1, November 25, 1998, p. 4401)

My mother was also known for her sense of humour and her writing abilities. Her writing skills and humour were on display in her political work, most memorably the time she wrote a parody of *'Twas the Night Before Christmas*, featuring her colleagues in the Nova Scotia House of Assembly.

While I wish she'd had more time to do the job she loved, I am happy Mom was able to do her dream job, even for four short years.

12. HELEN MACDONALD
NDP MLA FOR CAPE BRETON THE LAKES 1997–1999
Leader of the NDP 2000-2001

I was born in River Ryan, just outside the town of New Waterford, in a coal mining community. Coal miners were very active in the community, and my father was a long-time supporter of the CCF/ NDP. I was always aware of what was going on in my community. I graduated from college and got married, and my husband and I were very active in politics. When I was teaching and we lived in Inverness, there were not many New Democrats in the area. My husband and I and two or three others that were interested in the NDP used to paint our own signs when there would be an election. We did not always have a candidate, but we would paint and make our own signs, because there was no campaign or campaign teams available. We wanted people to realize that there were other options.

When we moved back to North Sydney, I had young children. But after my children began to grow up, my husband and I became very involved in the NDP party. I was principal at a school in Bras d'Or when I first ran. Alexa McDonough was a big influence in my life and in politics. Women in the NDP were very active, and very much engaged in what was going on. I became very active, serving in many positions in the local ridings here in Cape Breton and at the provincial level. My daughter was reminding me about those times the other day, she said: "I can remember when I was younger and you and dad and your NDP friends would be in the living room where you'd be having big discussions about one issue or another. We always heard the social democratic side of things." And that still influences her to this day.

I could not tell you how many times I ran before I was elected. It was probably at least five or six. I believed in what I was doing, and we had a good core of support here in my riding of Cape Breton the Lakes. It was always a learning experience, and it was work, but I really enjoyed doing it. You had to really learn how to balance your life—you are still an educator, a mother, and a wife when you run. But I was blessed in the fact that my husband was really engaged and was so supportive. As my children grew up, they were always dropping leaflets or doing something to help the campaigns. One of my daughters once said, "We were volun-told." But they were all happy to do it. I have five daughters, and one son. Especially with the girls, I think it was really, really important to engage them, because in the 70s and 80s girls weren't always the ones that were being engaged or expected to be engaged in politics.

It was November 1997 that I was first elected in a by-election. I was the first woman in Cape Breton to be elected provincially. Then, in 1998, I was re-elected. It was an amazing experience. I loved going door to door and talking to people. Even between campaigns, I always had community meetings. It was just so good to be out there in the community, listening to their stories and seeing how in some small way you can help people. Sometimes it was just a matter of listening.

I was defeated in 1999. There was a boardwalk being built in the area, and there were all kinds of concerns surrounding it. It was quite an issue in the community. I did a great deal of research and talked to those impacted. I became engaged in that issue, and some people were pleased I was doing what I believed to be the right thing to do, but other people were really, very angry. They thought I was going to be the one to destroy their opportunity to have a boardwalk. This was always a strong Liberal constituency, held by Bernie Boudreau for many years, and Progressive Conservative, John Newell as well. I know people must have thought, *what is she doing running against John Newell and Bernie Boudreau?* We were always friends in the end. But in the last campaign there was really a strong campaign to defeat me. The Liberals organized it. Many people I knew from the community and church, who were of course Liberals, wanted Brian Boudreau, the Liberal candidate to win, and he was elected. He won by a small majority. But a win is a win.

I was disappointed of course, but you know that is what can happen in politics. You go through the evaluation and the rehashing of what you could have done, but the bottom line is that the people made a decision. And the people are usually right. The school board had once been holding my position as director of curriculum for the district, but I knew that other people were carrying the load for me. I thought if I resigned, they would have someone replace me, which would be better for the educational system. I had tendered my resignation, and the next month I was defeated as a politician. It was what it was, but always when one door closes another one opens.

After that, I was blessed to have the opportunity to go to Africa and do volunteer work through the Canadian Teachers Federation as part of a team of teachers from Canada. That was a wonderful experience, and I never would have been able to do it if I was still a politician. I made thirteen trips back and forth to Africa over the years, working in deprived communities.

When I had made a few trips to Africa, I was encouraged by the team who had run my campaigns to run for leadership of the NDP party. I thought about it for a long time, and then I decided to do it. There were five of us who ran at that time, the only other woman was Maureen MacDonald. She continued on being an MLA and later became a minister—a very effective and knowledgeable politician. I won leadership, but I did not have a seat. There were many challenges to being able to lead without having a seat in the legislature. Some of the MLAs, especially some of the Liberal ones, could be very cruel at that time. They said I was "governing from the library," and there were lots of stories about me. But we worked through it with support from the party.

I still do not know whether it was the right decision or not, but a seat came available, and the party wondered whether I would consider running there. I think it was in Halifax Fairview. I was dead-set against it. My belief was that I should represent people in a community that I knew. I just felt in my soul the best thing for me to do was to run in Cape Breton. Cape Breton North came up, and I ran there. It was not far-fetched, as I had worked in Cape Breton North and taught there, and we lived there for many, many years. But I was soundly defeated. Cecil Clarke took the seat at that time.

That was the beginning of the end for my leadership. I did not have a seat, and I was not successful at winning a seat. It was no secret that there were some within the NDP caucus who were adamant that I leave. They were later referred to as 'the Cyanide Six.' I did not really get engaged one way or the other with them. I had been away on behalf of the party speaking somewhere, and on my way back, I was alone in the car and had a lot of time to think about it. I decided that I had no other choice, even though I would have loved to have continued, I just wasn't successful in elections. I stepped down.

I don't have any regrets. I was not engaged in politics much after I stepped down. I felt I needed to be away from it for a while. I would always campaign on behalf of someone else, but I never got engaged in the same way. I feel that I was lucky to have a lot of good support. I learned so much from Alexa McDonough and Eileen O'Connell. They were such good friends, and so valuable to the province. You learn and grow and do the best you can. And hopefully somewhere along the line you did something that helped somebody, or engaged somebody, or helped someone think, *if she can do it, I can do it.*

To me, you never change what you stand for or what you represent, but you always have to be considerate of the audience that is listening. I do not see any gain in a politician standing up and offending or bashing people that see differently from you. You have to engage the people. If you truly believe in what it is you are doing, and what you are standing for, you have to be able to get the people to understand that. They might not always agree with you, but you have to give them the respect they deserve to have their voices heard. That is who you are representing. You are representing the people who elected you.

I think women bring as much, and more, to the political scene as men. I do not mean to be unkind to men, but I think we have insights and feelings and can put ourselves in positions of other people for a better understanding. I think that is another level of thinking that we get more often in women. Women should feel there is no reason why we cannot contribute to politics.

There are so many stories from my time in politics, but to me, the best part of it was when you came back to your constituency and had the time to talk to other people that were not in Halifax sitting and hearing what was going on. To be able to relate it and apply it to their lives. I had people, as any politician would have, contacting me for things they needed. You always had a caseload. That was some of the more satisfying parts of the work. There were lots of cases—I remember trying to work through the challenges of helping a man get the eyeglasses he desperately needed, but could not afford, and the hurdles he faced. It was important to help, and at the same time maintain his dignity. There were so many individual and personal challenges people needed help and guidance with as they struggled through a not so friendly user system. That is the truly important work of a politician. It is the work in your constituency, the work on the ground that makes so much of a difference.

I have nine grandchildren. When I was involved in politics heavily, we were at a playground in North Sydney with my twin grandchildren. They were only small. Someone recognized the little guy and said, "What are you doing here in North Sydney?" He turned around and looked at her and said, "Oh, you must know my grandmother, Helen from the Lakes!" That is who I was. We had never really engaged them deeply in discussion of what I did, as they were so young. But he had picked up that I represented Cape Breton the Lakes—*Helen from the Lakes!*

Photo courtesy of Nova Scotia Legislature

13. The HONOURABLE MAUREEN MACDONALD
NDP MLA FOR HALIFAX NEEDHAM 1998–2016
Interim Leader of the New Democratic Party 2013–2016
First female Minister of Finance
Minister of Health

I am a social worker, and I have a Master of Social Work from Dalhousie University. Before running for office, I was a community legal worker at Dalhousie Legal Aid and had a very large caseload of teenage mothers. The Minister of Social Services at the time, Edmund Morris, decided to change the Social Assistance Act so that women between the ages of sixteen and eighteen who were mothers could not receive benefits. That resulted in quite a large confrontation between the government of the day and the legal clinic where I worked, and I was the face of that confrontation as a community activist.

    That planted the seed for me that political positions are powerful, and politicians make decisions that impact a lot of people. Although I really enjoyed representing people one-on-one, I really wanted to have the opportunity to make the structural changes that would affect a lot of people and improve their lives. Running politically was something I had thought about, but not in any real serious way. I decided you have to stand up and make your voice heard, and the political arena seemed to be the appropriate place. I was then approached by Alexa McDonough and the NDP to consider running. That made my decision easy.

I was elected in 1998, and a lot of barriers had been broken by that time. I benefitted as a woman enormously from the kinds of situations that women previous to me had found themselves in, particularly Alexa. She was the lone woman in the legislature for a period of time, and was also in a small party that had no other members. She was the only female member of her party. She had to fight to get a female washroom for female MLAs—otherwise she had to leave the chamber and go downstairs and use the public washroom. When I got there, those battles had happened. It was no longer peculiar, I would say, to have women members. I was elected with the largest female caucus that had ever happened at the time, with six women in our caucus in 1998. Parties were starting to look different.

I was always aware of the gendering of politics, and of the political context in which I operated in. But it was not a gross, overt, hostile environment. There was a lot of respect for women in our legislature by the time I got there. There was still gender politics, but it had stopped being overtly hostile and disrespectful. I was able to focus on the things I went there to do, rather than just protect myself all the time from that kind of violent sexism.

Generally speaking, the gender relations were better than they had been in the fifteen years preceding my time in the legislature. But female MLAs still have to deal with the public, and that is where the real difference comes in. Women MLAs are treated tremendously differently by some members of the public than male MLAs. Men probably are not called 'honey,' and don't get comments on how they look all the time. If you go on the six o'clock news for an interview, I'm sure men are not getting comments about why they didn't bring a hairbrush. There is still a lot of misogyny there, and female MLAs tend to be the focal point of that.

Every time women occupy different positions of authority, they experience gender relations either overtly or subtly. That would show up in different ways when I became the Minister of Health, and then later the Minister of Finance. As Health Minister, I tried to be very aware of the gender relations inside the groups I was working in and tried to hear the lived experiences of women in those professions.

Finance was a whole other world. In our world, I think finance is dominated by men. It is seen as a hard science, which it is not. It was fascinating for me to go from the health portfolio to finance, because in health you are constantly dealing with emotional situations. They were life and death, gut wrenching kinds of cases. Our healthcare system is constantly under pressure and scrutinized in that context—in the context of people. Are you a caring minister? Are you aware of the human dimensions, the emotional dimensions, the impact of people not getting care? And then I got into the department of finance where being emotional was like blasphemy. There is no emotion in the department, it is all cold, calculated scientifically based questions.

And yet everyone thinks that getting the finance portfolio is a promotion, that you have the 'tough' job. To me, that was so wrong. Finance was an easier department in many ways. My predecessor in finance was Graham Steele, and he used to joke about it with me. We sat side by side in the House of Assembly as ministers, and for question period we had briefing books which we called a 'hot book'— it was the topics of the day we thought might come up at question period. Graham would come in with his briefing book with basically nothing in it, and I was there with the health book with pages and pages and pages of information. He would pop his open to show me there was nothing there and give me a giant grin.

The Minister of Health got three thousand pieces of correspondence a month. Finance probably gets that in a year. I think that the perception of it being a better or harder job comes from the idea that working with people is not as important and not as difficult as working with the hard numbers. It is very gendered. It's like the caring side of the world—taking care of kids, taking care of your elderly parents, keeping a household going, cooking the meals, all of those things are a piece of cake. No skills involved. The skills are seen to be over on the financial side, the side with no emotion. It was fascinating for me to have that experience of doing both.

There were many things we accomplished in my time in office that I am proud of. When I was Minister of Health, I worked on the first and the only mental health strategy for the province. My best day in government was announcing a five-year plan to improve mental health services. In that plan was something called peer support and peer counselling. In Canada at the time, it was a new idea that people with mental illness who had been successfully treated could work with people who were starting to experience recovery. This has grown tremendously. The professional side of the field now recognizes the value of peer support.

In opposition, I introduced a bill that the government was willing to adopt—the Protection for Persons in Care Act. It is a piece of legislation that requires facilities where vulnerable people are patients or residents to report instances of abuse. It systematized the scrutiny and accountability for the quality of care. I do not think the Act has been updated. When you introduce legislation, you are opening the door with the knowledge that it is not a perfect piece of legislation, but you get the framework in place. You hope it will be improved on as it is operationalized, and you realize what the gaps are.

When the NDP was in opposition, and the government was the John Hamm government, we were able to develop an entire campaign that forced the Hamm government to change health policy so that anyone in the province who required long term care would not have to liquidate their assets. Long term care in Nova Scotia became essentially part of the public system, in a semi-universal way. This is another thing that needs to be expanded on—but seeing the expansion of medicare as a New Democrat was also a really important achievement. And we did it from the opposition bench, with a lot of hard work.

The world has gotten tougher and rougher in my view. I look at today's world, and I wonder if I would want to do what I did today. I told a colleague of mine before she ran that this is not a glamorous job. You need to come into it with your eyes wide open. There are opportunities to make a real difference, and to work on some things that you would really like to see changed. But there is a cost for doing that. To be good at this job, you have to work 24/7. You have no personal life. You are opening yourself up to be scrutinized and criticized for everything from the way you dress, how you look, how you speak, the model of car you drive, where you go, and who you hang out with.

For me, I had a great experience. I do not have a lot of regrets. In life, that is not a bad place to be when you are sixty-five and retired. I learned tremendously. You will never find an environment where you have such a learning opportunity. If you are a person who thrives on constant change and information and learning, it is amazing. You are learning all the time how things actually work. And the people you meet make it great. People are truly phenomenal.

When I was first elected, I noticed when I would be with other MLAs, they would say, "I didn't get into this to be a goddamn social worker." I was so offended by this. I saw the work I did as an MLA as an extension of the social work I did years ago. Over time, I heard this so many times from members of all parties. What they were expressing was they did not want to have to deal with people's problems. They did not want people coming to them and asking them for help with an issue or problem. That made me crazy—social work was the profession I chose to go into, where people would come to you and ask for assistance. As MLAs I thought, *what a privilege it is for people to perceive you as someone they can turn to with their most serious problems and issues.* You can't always help or change what they present, but often you can. And that is an honourable thing.

14. YVONNE ATWELL
NDP MLA for Preston 1998–1999
First African Nova Scotian woman elected to the Nova Scotia legislature

I was born in East Preston, Nova Scotia, during the middle of the Second World War. I sometimes think that those of us born during this time had a particular purpose that led us to larger visions for community, even though we did not know it at the time. At the age of seventeen, I left Nova Scotia and moved to Toronto to live with my sister. Leaving home at such a young age presented me with many challenges but I quickly realized that I needed to continue my education. I spent the first years working and upgrading my education, taking courses at the community college and university in community development and management. I was always driven to do what I needed to do to upgrade myself and my education.

I moved back to Nova Scotia in 1989, where I built my house in East Preston. When I looked around the community, I could see that a lot had not really changed so I started volunteering and getting involved in community initiatives. I became a member of the board at the Black United Front and worked with some youth who wanted to build a ball field at our local recreation centre. It was because I was active in the community that I ended up meeting Alexa McDonough at a local community barbeque and after a lengthy discussion she asked me if I would be interested in running for the NDP; initially I had said no but after having many more conversations I finally made a decision to run.

It was through Alexa's encouragement that my political journey began. The support of family, friends, and many community members were crucial for me. My father's support was particularly special as he was a staunch Liberal, but he voted for the NDP in support of me anyway; this was and still is a source of pride for me. My father was such a strong family man who was always there for me and his support meant a lot. Once the decision was made, I just jumped right in and did what was needed as I was determined to win. I was focused and stayed committed; running three times before I won. I also ran for leadership of the NDP during that time.

Did I experience sexism and racism? Yes, that was a given as a politician. Those are some of the first things you have to think about when you are elected. I experienced all kinds of discrimination as a Black woman. People would ask me questions like, "What makes you so smart? Why do you think you could do this? Why run? You don't know the issues."

These issues were especially prominent when I ran for leadership of the NDP. I ran in the leadership race in 1996 that elected Robert Chisholm as leader. I had not won a seat as MLA at that time, but I decided to try for the leadership position anyway. I travelled across the province picking up a lot of support, but I also picked up a lot of views like, *who are you?* People discounted me and did not take me seriously, while others helped with fundraising and were supportive. I did not expect this to be an easy ride, but hard work never scared me—I felt the fear and did it anyway.

When I went to the NDP leadership convention, it was intimidating; it was a large convention and I was very nervous approaching the podium to make my speech. I had a moment when I lost my place while speaking but I did not panic, I found the page and continued. I remember that moment because it showed me that even though I knew I was not going to win I could stand my ground. I even picked up 20 percent of the vote. After that convention, I felt I had enough support to run for MLA in the Preston riding again in 1998 and I won! Before I knew it, I was in the House of Assembly; the first Black woman to be elected as an MLA in Atlantic Canada.

When I look back, I am proud of the fact that I was able to represent the community and talk about the things I thought were important to them and work on their behalf when I was in the House. I am proud that I could build relationships across the aisle, advocating and helping my community. It was, and still is, important that the community is aware of the developments that take place in the Nova Scotia House of Assembly and that my efforts on their behalf were not in vain.

Being a woman, and the only Black woman in the House, you have to suffer through that alone; I needed more Black people around me, so I insisted we have a Black researcher and staff person. Discrimination came in many forms—people would not sit with me in the cafeteria at the House. I remember once I was standing in line for lunch and picked up a banana, and one man said to me, "Oh, you like bananas, huh? Wayne Adams liked bananas, too."[6] A few male members would sit across the aisle in the House and would try and stare me down. But I felt that we had a good strong team in our caucus; this helped me get through some of the negatives.

I have talked to several young women, and their concern about politics is they think that they are unable to succeed. But when you look at some of the men who are successful in politics, they may not

---

[6] Wayne Adams was the first Black member of the Nova Scotia House of Assembly.

have those doubts, and really? Women doubt themselves even when they are more than qualified. I talk to people, especially Black women, who have a lot of doubts about themselves. As young women we often feel this way as, if some areas of work are just not possible. I would advise many women, whenever I had an opportunity to just step out and do it—if nothing else the experience is worth it. I would encourage them to take a look at all political parties and figure out their most important values and principles.

It is also very important to gather support around you before you step out. When I ran, I won the nomination for my riding by only one or two votes. My daughter, a young NDP who was only around seventeen at the time, had brought out her friends to ensure that I would get that nomination. It really can come down to simple things like who you can get to show up and support you. After winning the nomination so closely, and basically from the support of those who knew my daughter, I realized that this can happen for anyone. But you have to build your team early. You must do the work ahead of time—especially for us, when you want to represent Black communities. You have to make sure people will show up and support you.

I would tell people, especially young Black women, there is a place for you in the legislature. But you cannot be afraid of it, you will run into sexism and racism. You have to know that and be prepared to deal with it. There is no reason young people cannot run for politics. What you do not already know, you can learn, and you will learn fast. I am still very excited about politics. I would support any woman who was interested, especially in the Preston community as this is where representation is needed.

15. ROSEMARY GODIN
NDP MLA FOR SACKVILLE-BEAVER BANK 1998–1999

My background is in journalism. I had my degree in English and a diploma in journalism. I wrote about Bedford, Sackville, and Hammonds Plains, and I covered a lot of politics. I had a career for about fifteen to twenty years, and you were never really allowed to have an opinion on anything—which I did not. But after a while, you begin to see that there are needs in the community. Frankly, I had not really thought about running until John Holm, who was an NDP MLA, asked me if I would consider it. The first thing I said was, "No, I can't do that!" It took a few weeks of thinking about it. Then I thought, *Why not?* I think above all, I decided to do it because I was a woman. There were so few female voices at that time. I had come up through the era of Alexa McDonough—and what an inspiration she was for so many women in this province.

In my time in office, I was able to work directly on one of my passions—affordable housing. I was the Opposition Critic for Housing and Residential Tenancies during my tenure. Recently, in Sydney, I was the only woman sitting on a small community committee that worked with the government for two years to get the first homeless shelter for women and youth built, as well as an updated men's shelter, in downtown Sydney. The shelter opened in late 2019.

There were things about politics that were not pleasant. Fortunately, there were five women in our caucus. There were six in total (in the House), with one Liberal across the floor, Francene Cosman. We really stuck together because we had to. That is another reason why more women should run—because you really need each other. There is strength in numbers. They made fun of us often. I have always had a voice disability. They liked to make up names for people, and I was Marge from *The Simpsons* because of my voice. There were also a lot of cat calls and stuff back then. It was not a female-friendly place to be.

As women, we brought up Alexa McDonough a lot because she had only been leader a few years before. Some of the guys would say, "Forget about Alexa McDonough! She is in the past, she is gone. We have to talk about now." Well, to the women, she was a really important figure. She was probably the reason that almost every one of us was sitting there. It was not always pleasant because it seemed like, and it was said, that the men's power was a very intangible power. It was intangible, but there. Women have a different approach. As the years go on, I see more women getting into politics and I see what [Justin] Trudeau did with the gender balanced cabinet, and that makes me feel very hopeful.

I do believe that almost everyone goes into politics wanting to help. I may have stars in my eyes.

Back then, an MLA only made about $45,000 a year. I was uncomfortable when one of the first things we did behind closed doors in caucus was to vote ourselves a 6 percent raise. I spoke out against it, because at the same time we were doing that, there were people in public service picketing outside Province House looking for a raise, early retirement, and a new contract. And we were back there voting to give ourselves a 6 percent raise. I said, "This is not right."

I was told, "Oh some of you have come in, and this is a pay raise for you." I knew they were talking about me, because I was a single mom raising two kids working on a newspaper. I wasn't making $45,000 at that time. But they said, "A lot of us have had to take a pay cut from our private sector positions. If it really bothers you, Rosemary, you can just give your 6 percent away to charity."

We would walk into caucus behind closed doors, and there was especially one male MLA who kept reminding us that politics was like a hockey game. He would come in and would announce that we were either playing defence or we were playing forward.

We were official opposition, which gives you the feeling that you are really close to power, so if there was a problem to be fixed it was like, "Oh forget about that. Put that aside! We'll do that when we get the power." It was a grab for power rather than seeing if you could get together with the Liberals or the Conservatives to actually fix what needed to be fixed. I think it is probably difficult for a lot of women to play that kind of politics.

Constituency office work was where you get to be yourself and help folks out. I found the office work to be so gratifying for myself and my wonderful female assistant, Brenda Haley. People would come to our office, and together we worked at helping people. It was very satisfying to be able to help them find a way around things, and to help empower people. Even before I went into politics, I had been considering going into church work to become a minister. When I ran for MLA, I kind of put that aside because I did not really think I was going to win. But I won, so that put a hold on the rest of my life for a while. I had wanted to go back to school and get my Masters in Divinity, which I have since done. Being an MLA really solidified that in myself. It is really public service. My father and my grandfather were both in politics, so community service was very much in my environment. I knew the importance of it. I knew when I came out of politics that I was making the right decision going into the church because it was just a continuum—it was a way of helping people. In that way, politics really solidified that I wanted to continue my life in a way that served my community.

As for young women, I would tell them to by all means do it, because we need you. We definitely need the female, and youth, voices in the halls of power.

16. MARY ANN MCGRATH
PC MLA FOR HALIFAX BEDFORD BASIN 1999–2003

Growing up, I had a wonderful role model in my father who treated us all the same. He did not presuppose that boys did one thing and girls did another. I never felt different, or disadvantaged, or limited. I assumed that if I think I can do it, I can. When I was a kid and I was complaining about something, my father would say, "Well what are you going to do about it? If you are going to complain you have to do something about it, or you have to be quiet." Well, I cannot be quiet, so I guess that was the beginning of a lifetime of sticking my nose into things.

I am a property paralegal; I do property law for a living. But what led me into politics was being a PTA chair, a school education activist, and community shit-disturber. When I became active in my children's schools through the PTA, there was so much idiocy in the bureaucratic decisions being made. We had a department of education that justified their existence by turning out more programming and textbooks and learning plans...but the money never followed to the schools to buy the books, to buy the programming, to re-educate the teachers on how to teach it. By the time the PTA raised the money to do it, the department had moved on to the next thing. It was such a waste. Trying to fix problems after they happen made me think it would be more sensible to go higher up the food chain. I finally realized if I wanted to make real changes, I had to go where the changes originated. And that was the legislature.

I had always felt that politics, particularly elected politics, belonged to educated people. I had part of a commerce degree, but I did not have the whole thing. It finally occurred to me that my local politician was a sports newscaster, so was there really much difference between his experience and mine? I thought, *I'm sure a Paralegal is just as smart as a sportscaster—no disrespect to sportscasters.* I began to realize that politics was quickly becoming a world where it was not just lawyers and doctors filling the seats, there were all kinds of people. Luckily the riding association agreed with me. They test ran me as president first, and then agreed to support me for the nomination.

I had a wonderful caucus. Our caucus had a highway supervisor, a truck driver, a minister, business owners, and only one lawyer. John Hamm was our premier. There were three women in our caucus, and none of us were wallflowers. Honestly, I did not feel any different than anybody else. It was pointed out to me during the 1999 campaign that I was the first woman to ever run in that riding, and my response was, "So?"

In the 2003 election, there were three women running in my riding and everyone was saying, "This has never happened in Nova Scotia!" My response again was, "So?" People asked me if I was pleased to see this happen, and I thought, *'I will be pleased to see it when you stop talking about it. Because this should not still be abnormal, different or unusual.'* If we stop talking about it like it's abnormal, it will become normal.

Politics was a whirlwind. It is a very intense job, a 24/7 job. You go to the grocery store at eleven o'clock at night, and people stop you in the aisle. You have to know a little bit about a lot of things, and be willing to listen and learn. You very quickly figure out what is realistic, what you can say to people, and what you cannot. You do not want to raise people's hopes unnecessarily, but at the same time be realistic and supportive of the things that are important to people.

You learn to really depend on good girlfriends to keep your feet on the ground. When I see people commenting on decisions like, "What did he do that for, is he crazy? What were they thinking?" They do not realize politicians are in a bubble. We are in a tightly closed bubble with all of these folks around us advising us on appropriate action. If we are not careful, we can forget our own instincts and our own common sense. I really struggled with that. My girlfriends used to say, "Tonight you are coming out to dinner with us, and that is your appointment tonight." That helped bring me back to reality.

There were also excellent mentors within politics. People in our caucus were wonderful, but also outside of our caucus. Maureen MacDonald was an exceptional mentor. Even a few members of the Liberal Party, after they tried to bust my chops and challenge me and I would not back down; they decided I was worth the trouble. I tried to take cues from anybody who seemed to have a sensible opinion, approach, or advice. One requirement of the job is you have to have good people instincts so you can trust who you are listening to. And trust who you should ignore and politely dismiss. It is an extremely different world, it cannot be compared to anything, and I have done a number of things in my life.

I am proud of the Blue Mountain Birch Cove Lakes Wilderness Area. It will be there long after I am gone. Programs and legislation, those things can be undone or superseded, but that physical ground of the Wilderness Area is not going anywhere. I also had success with advocating for local schools—the new Halifax West High School, new Park West School, that was very satisfying for an education activist!

Inside our government, I fought for improved support for women in crisis—changes to policies like the Domestic Violence Act, that said the husband must be the one to leave the house in those situations.

Policies that were common sense and fair. But that is legislation, it comes and goes and gets changed. Program funding gets changed. You really make big changes when you make changes in consciousness. We were the first government to recognize same sex marriage. We could not make it legal because that is a federal responsibility, so we came up with the Domestic Partnership Act. You could register any relationship at the Vital Statistics Office, and it stands to this day. It was ground-breaking at the time. Things like that changed a mood, and even if someone changed legislation after that, we had changed the way things are done and thought about.

My advice would be pay attention to your inner voice. Decide who you are, and why you want to do this. This year, 2019, we just came out of a federal election, and we never heard one leader of any party say why they wanted or deserved to be prime minister of this country. Know why you want to do it. Know what you can bring to the table, know what you are fighting for. Have some clear goals on what you want to accomplish, and what you see that you want to help fix. And then go and do it. Folks like me, call us up and ask us questions.

I did not let anyone inside or outside of my caucus tell me what I should feel or think. If I had an opinion, I said it. I said it in caucus, I said it to my coworkers, I said it to the press, and I said it to constituents. I was never politically correct. I can't be, it's not in my DNA. If you asked me a question, I would tell you the truth, even when someone would tell me I couldn't say it. I was never cruel, I don't think I ever intentionally shatter peoples' dreams, but if someone brought something to me, I would be honest. I want people to feel I was honest, I didn't sugar coat things, and that I tried my best.

Jane Purves on the day she was sworn in as MLA for Halifax-Citadel.
Photos courtesy of her son and daughter-in-law, Tom and Kristen.

17. The HONOURABLE JANE PURVES (1949 – 2013)
PC MLA FOR HALIFAX-CITADEL 1999–2003
First female Minister of Health
First female Minister of Education

This excerpt is taken from an interview with Tom and Kristen, Jane's son and daughter-in-law.

My mother, Jane Purves, is an absolutely fascinating figure. Her family lived in the South End, and she had many opportunities growing up. Her parents were very focused on the success of their children, and gave them the best education. My mother was very smart. She went to the Ladies' College in Halifax, which is now Armbrae Academy. My uncle made a comment in her obituary, "There is only one prize she didn't win there. That is second place." She got all the top awards. I still have her report cards—she was a prodigy. She graduated when she was sixteen, and then went to Dalhousie [University].

When you have girls that are so smart, but somewhat bridled, they rebel. My mom did that. She had a rebellious phase in the late '60s and '70s. She dealt with addiction to drugs. But she always did very well and was very involved. She did a lot of neat things and worked cool jobs, like working in a record store.

She worked hard and changed her life, and almost immediately after she did she got involved in journalism. She was highly capable and an amazing writer. She worked her way up in the *Chronicle Herald* organization, at that time for the Dennis family. I always remember this note from Sarah Dennis about the impact that my mother had on her. She really had an impact on the other professional women in her life. If you want to know her story, I think it comes out in the women she influenced. When I think back to the days in the *Herald* newsroom, I do not think she realized how much of an impact she was having on the people there. She really impacted many lives and many young women.

She spent a long time at the *Herald*, covering a lot of different beats. She worked her way up, starting in Truro covering rural news, and advancing quickly. She was sent to cover Quebec in the '70s and all the radical changes that were happening there. I think that forged a lot of her really intense feelings about politics. She took a stint at CBC for a while and had her own show there. Later, after her time in politics, she went back and became a political commentator and used many of those skills.

When her journalism career ended, someone convinced her that she should run as part of the John Hamm government, so that is what she did. She certainly had no expectation that she would be successful, but she did have a strong connection to the riding she ran in in the South End. The family was all involved in her campaign. She was a hard-worker and she grinded during that election. She got out in every neighbourhood and talked to every person. I think she won some hearts and minds. It was an NDP riding, but it was time for a change, and she had the personality as well as the background knowledge to speak on any issue. She had the right team around her. It all coalesced at the right moment and she won that election. I remember being with the whole family on election night watching the results come in.

Just like that she was off to caucus and off to cabinet. She was initially the Minister of Health, and then she was shuffled into education. Those really were the hardest portfolios, and I think that showed their confidence in her. She had really good advisors, and she knew the issues really well. But there is a mechanics to politics that make you successful in the long term. It is about the long game—being practical and not idealistic. And Mom was idealistic. Her downfall in education was making a call about LeMarchant-St. Thomas School in the South End. It was in her riding. It was an interesting position for her to be in, because the school was in her riding, but she was also the Minister of Education. It forced her to decide between those two roles. It was a situation where the best decision was not politically safe. You do the right thing, but you do not always survive it. She was principled, and the principle here was that if you were going to treat everyone fairly, then the right thing to do was close the school. That was the anchor that took her down in the election in 2003.

After her election loss, she was hired as Chief of Staff. She worked for John Hamm and then Jamie Baillie. She ran a tight ship. You get a call from Jane, and you would never end up arguing with her. She could checkmate you pretty quickly. She had quite a long run at that, all the way into her sixties. However, politics is a 24/7 job. It wears you down.

When retirement came, she was just very excited to just be a grandmother. My wife and I had two young children. We were living in the Hydrostone, and our neighbours' home went up for sale. We asked her if she would come be close to us, and she did. When we moved to another house, she was thinking, *Do I want to be a grandmother, or do I want to live a more fun lifestyle?* She contemplated moving in with my aunt, but she decided that she wanted to stay close to our girls and bought a place right by our home now.

She loved the opportunity to develop a relationship with her son, and with our family. She loved living near us, and she could not resist being there with her granddaughters as they grew up. We are so thankful we had her nearby during those years. What a gift to our girls. We would get home, and would not even come into our house—they would run right over to hers. It was like they had two homes.

She used to take our daughters out to lunch, and our oldest was just four years old, and she would take her for latkes and smoked salmon. She cultivated a taste for caviar in our two year old! She treated our girls like gold. She was someone who could be so brilliant, but also so loving. When I think about the way she was with our girls, and with us, and she had so many great friends, it is just evident how much people loved her.

She had the most amazing relationship with her mother's mother. I don't know a lot about Ellen Purves, but she was another very accomplished woman. She graduated from the University of New Brunswick in 1908, as far as I know, she was the first woman to receive a master's degree from the university. My mom spent a lot of time with Ellen before she passed away. Because of her own relationship with her grandmother, where she was treated like gold, I think that was passed into my mother's relationship with our children.

At the end of her life, she started to wind down and do some travelling. She went on a safari in South Africa and explored the Caribbean. She went to London to spend some time. But within a year and a half of her cancer diagnosis, she passed away.

My mom was many things. I still do not know anyone who can do a *New York Times* crossword puzzle faster than her. She was a really good gift giver. She was always aware of the culture and what was happening; she was hip. She had a huge library. When she passed away, the biggest task we had to do was pack up her books and catalogue them. It took three months to do it. And she had read every one of those books, some many times. I think if she had found a way to make it profitable, she would have opened a bookstore. She would sometimes start writing books herself but would never actually finish. I still have these fragments of stories she wrote, I found them stashed as bookmarks in some of her books.

There was something unusual about her. More than anything, it was her ability for her to be herself for her entire life. It was her intellect and raw capability to outperform other people, mostly men. But the impact she had on other women is really her story. She had challenges, and she broke through all of them. They had a positive impact on her life in terms of who she was able to impact and what she was able to accomplish. She was a blazing example of how strong and how smart women can be.

Photo courtesy of Deborah Baillie

18. MURIEL BAILLIE (1935 – 2018)
PC MLA FOR PICTOU WEST 1999–2003

This excerpt is written by Muriel's daughter, Deborah Baillie.

Not many people would be able to successfully navigate politics while carrying the nickname Fluff, but Muriel Unice Baillie did. Her father bestowed the nickname upon her a few days after her birth, and she used it throughout her life. During her career in education which began in 1954, from teaching in one-room schoolhouses and later, elementary classrooms and a principalship, there were many students, parents, friends, and neighbours who never even knew she was actually named Muriel. Not wanting to lose her name recognition nor to appear to suddenly be someone she was not, Muriel bravely ventured into politics identified as Fluff.

By the time Fluff had retired from education in 1991, she had also spent twelve years helping to manage the sawmill operation run by her husband. Always active behind the scenes, Fluff had never given any thought to entering electoral politics herself. However in 1999, when no local candidate was forthcoming, and with encouragement from her husband and the local steering committee, Fluff allowed her name to go forward for the Progressive Conservative nomination.

Not having experience on the political front lines, Fluff met the challenge of getting elected as she had all previous challenges: with dedication, energy, hard work, and teamwork. As she had many times in her earlier endeavours, she acquired whatever additional skills were needed only after undertaking the new commitment, effectively always learning on the job. In fact, learning was a way of life for Fluff, whether it was in education, politics, or her personal life. She was often heard to remark, "It's a poor day when you don't learn something."

Fluff was an energetic, vibrant person with a ready smile and engaging laugh who loved being with people and could light up a room. Not the first woman candidate in Pictou West, she was, however, the first for the Progressive Conservative Association, and the first female MLA for the riding, one of only three women elected to the legislative assembly at the time. She was well aware of the fact that only a very small number of people had ever had the privilege to serve as the MLA and never took her position for granted. Although she would have liked to have seen more women candidates at all levels of government and more women MLAs, she did not dwell on the gender imbalance, preferring instead to simply focus on the task at hand and work collaboratively within the male-dominated field.

Fluff was very proud of her community, her county, and her province, and had great respect for the workings of government and the traditions of the legislative assembly. She considered it an honour to represent and serve the residents of Pictou West under Premier Hamm's leadership, advocating for more provincial funding for transportation, healthcare, and education. She had a passion for helping people and derived great pleasure from addressing the needs of individuals. She never thought she had all the answers but was always willing to listen to her constituents and ask on their behalf, whatever questions it took to resolve their issues.

Shortly after being elected, Fluff's personal life was turned upside down by the death of her husband whom she described as her 'number one supporter.' She completed her term in office and chose not to stand for re-election in 2003, instead stepping away from public life to spend time with her family.

Retiring from politics, Fluff knew her life had been enriched by the many great and extraordinary people she had met under many different circumstances. The one regret she expressed was that she had started her political career too late in life to be able to continue representing the wonderful people of Pictou West. Never having lost her sense of humour or joy of life, she would have agreed that there will be many MLAs but there would only ever be one Fluff.

19. JOAN MASSEY
NDP MLA FOR DARTMOUTH EAST 2003-2009

Joan Massey was a Member of the Nova Scotia House of Assembly, representing the riding of Dartmouth East for the New Democratic Party from 2003–2009. She was born in Dartmouth, Nova Scotia, and attended school there. Before politics, she worked as an administrative assistant and office manager, and serves as vice president of a family owned and operated company.

From 1997–2000, she was an elected member of the Halifax Regional School Board. She won the 2003 election, the 2006 election, and was defeated in the 2009 election.

She did not participate in this book.[7]

---

[7] This information was adapted from "Nova Scotia NDP biography", archived from 2003.

Photo courtesy of NSCC from Marilyn More

20. The HONOURABLE MARILYN MORE
NDP MLA FOR DARTMOUTH SOUTH-PORTLAND VALLEY 2003-2013
Minister of Education and Early Childhood Development, Labour and Workforce Development, and Volunteerism
Minister of Labour and Advanced Education, Immigration and the Status of Women
Minister responsible for the Public Service Commission, Communications Nova Scotia and the Status of Women

My background is really in community volunteerism, starting as a young student in Dartmouth. I trained to be a teacher originally but I only taught junior high for two years, and then I left to raise my children. When I was home with my two young sons, I became more involved in community organizations. Early on I became a member of the Dartmouth club of the Canadian Federation of University Women (CFUW). One of their projects was sending an observer to all the Dartmouth school board meetings who reported back so that members could stay informed and better promote progressive education. I attended school board meetings for over five years in this observer role. At that time, the school board was half municipal politicians appointed by city council and half provincial appointees appointed by the provincial government. Our club was part of a movement trying to encourage more women appointees with the long term goal of having fully elected school boards in Nova Scotia.

In 1978, the provincial government decided to have one-third of each school board elected. And the elections were going to be held at the same time as the municipal elections. As chance would have it, Dartmouth was the first municipality to have an election that fall. Because the CFUW had been pushing both inclusive membership and ultimately fully elected school boards, they very much wanted to support a woman candidate and who better, they reasoned, than one of their own members. In their eyes, I seemed a natural—knew the local public education issues, trained as a teacher, was a regular school board meeting attendee, shared their views on progressive curriculum and programs, was a mother of young children and so on. I was stunned at the suggestion, but the more I discussed the possibility with them, the more I realized I had an opportunity to turn advocacy into action. The CFUW and many friends and neighbours got behind me, as well as my amazing family, and we put on a city-wide campaign for this young mom. And I won. I actually came in second in total votes to Dr. John Savage, which made me the first woman to be elected to a school board in Nova Scotia.

Just to give you an example of the challenge at that time, there were seventeen or eighteen people offering for the four elected seats available. Many were well-known professionals and business people. It was a city-wide election, no districts. There was an initial newspaper article highlighting Dr. Savage and his many achievements, as well as covering a number of the better known business people running. In this lengthy article, the last sentence was, "And several housewives are also offering." No names, no background, nothing. Just 'several housewives.'

It was an amazing ten years on the school board. I learned so much about the political process, basically how decisions were made, in addition to engaging with and respecting citizens and staff, building support for new initiatives and change, remaining true to my personal values, doing my own research and especially putting children first. After ten years, I realized it was time to refresh the school board leadership and pursue another direction, so I did not offer for a fourth term and got involved in community social development.

A three-year, federally-funded rural social development initiative called Challenge in Participation, under the sponsorship of the Anglican Diocese of Nova Scotia (and PEI), the Nova Scotia Victorian Order of Nurses and the Palliative Care Association of Nova Scotia, gave me another life-changing opportunity. The provincial organization (called Community Links) grew out of the project and I became the executive director for the first eleven years. Through volunteer development and mainly senior leadership, rural organizations developed and supported volunteer-based programs for local seniors, persons with disabilities and rural communities across the province, including the Falls Prevention Network. Community Links celebrated its twenty-fifth anniversary in 2017 and continues strong.

I joined the NDP around 1997 after meeting a number of members when presenting a session about Community Links at a Topshee Conference at St. Francis Xavier in Antigonish. The participants came from various backgrounds and discussed social and economic issues impacting Atlantic Canada. I was hooked, and thoroughly enjoyed the topics and speakers as well as the camaraderie. It was a stage in my life when I had time, energy, and ongoing passion for social justice to offer my service, and within a few years I became provincial party president.

As president I was particularly involved with encouraging more women and visible minorities to offer as candidates in the 2003 provincial election. A couple of friends and party members asked, "Have you ever considered running?" I had community experience, understood the issues and political process, and had even declined all three major parties to run for them earlier in my life. Once again, I was taken aback by the very suggestion. Part of me cringed at the idea of putting myself out publicly like that. But I thought perhaps I do have something to offer at this stage of my life. I was particularly motivated to push for lifelong learning and senior and voluntary sector supports. The timing was fortunate—my children were grown, I did not have senior caregiving responsibilities at that point, just my beloved duck toller, so I decided to take the plunge.

I have to say winning the initial NDP nomination was tougher for me than winning the seat in the provincial election—the nomination was initially a tie. A former well-respected NDP MLA from this area decided to offer again after losing the previous election. I felt badly about challenging him, but I believed we needed more women in decision-making circles and continued with the nomination race. I actually won on the toss of a coin. So pure chance and luck played a huge role in winning the nomination. I went on to become the MLA for Dartmouth South-Portland Valley in the 2003 provincial election after a strong NDP team effort.

Ten years as MLA was one adventure after another. Hurricane Juan hit Nova Scotia shortly after I was elected. I remember driving around the constituency, meeting groups of neighbours helping each other among scenes of unbelievable destruction. During my first term, I joined other citizens working on lakes protection (Dartmouth Area Waterways Network) and social issues and programs (Public Good Society of Dartmouth). I had an interesting variety of caucus responsibilities while in opposition and served on several House of Assembly committees. Then the election of 2009 took place, and suddenly I was a government cabinet minister—a roller coaster of experiences over four years. I felt honoured to be able to serve my province in this way. I literally pinched myself under the table in several situations, never having imagined my community involvement would lead to this!

I do not feel comfortable discussing many of the challenges and barriers to women in politics. Some are not my stories to tell, although I witnessed them, and I prefer to focus on the many people and acts of generosity that helped me along the way. I did not face as many barriers as some women elected to other school boards did, even in the 1980s. Dartmouth has always been progressive, and I have to give credit to the women and men elected and appointed with me on those school boards and the professional and teaching staff for the level of mutual respect and support.

But I remember going to a provincial conference shortly after I was elected to the school board in 1978, and for some reason I was a little late (blame it on the traffic) and the first session had already started. I walked into the room that I thought had been listed, and this sea of men glanced at me. I backed out of the room, thinking I must have been in the wrong room. I started towards the hotel lobby desk to check where I should be, and this woman came running out and she said, "Are you Marilyn? You were in the right room; we are waiting for you!"

She was actually the president of the School Boards Association at the time. But almost every other person in that room was a man. Over the years it became more balanced, but certainly in the early days it was very male-dominated. It was not surprising that local committee meetings were usually over lunch and supper times—always problematic for a mom with young children.

Reflecting back, I realize that often women in politics are sometimes 'invisible'—not listened to as carefully or their suggestions taken as seriously as their male colleagues. So we had to be strategic, well-researched and, at times, determined to promote our ideas and solutions.

I am a strong believer in personal values driving my beliefs and actions. To me, you get more out of life and you get further towards your goals if you care about your family, friends, and community, you get involved, work hard, and respect others. If you base your life, career, relationships, and aspirations on those values, you can't go wrong. I am so grateful to my family, friends, party members, political and community colleagues and constituents for the support and encouragement they have given me my entire life. I know the wonderful opportunities I had, and there have been many, would not have been possible without them.

21. MICHELE RAYMOND
NDP MLA FOR HALIFAX ATLANTIC 2003–2013

I grew up in Nova Scotia, though my parents were not from here. My father was an American and my mother was Bermudian; they were academics who came to Nova Scotia in the early 1960s. I was educated here and at Yale, and later studied law at Dalhousie, although that has not been my vocation. I have actually worked as an editor most of my life, and before I stood for office, was at home raising children and initiating various projects that I felt would assist with life in my particular community, which was rapidly changing.

I am not naturally a particularly outspoken person. In fact, I would say I was pathologically shy as a child, but later, there were community issues that I felt needed to be addressed.

By 2003, I had been working for several years on what I thought of as an Urban Farm Museum, which I wanted to see started in Spryfield, so as to restore traditional local food production and skills, and in 2001 and 2002 I had run a pilot project operating a peak time ferry service across the Northwest Arm. I did these things because no one else was doing them.

In late 2002 I was working on a book on the history of the Northwest Arm with another author. During that time I was approached by the NDP, asking whether I would run to replace Robert Chisholm in Halifax Atlantic. My initial response was, "No way." I was sure I would lose friends and frankly, respect. We had a family friend who used to say about one of her neighbours, that he was like a mosquito: as soon as anyone opened the door, he would get in the house and she could not get rid of him. That is how I thought about politicians.

The NDP approached me again six months later, when the book was largely finished, and this time I mentioned the idea to a friend. She was not a close friend, but someone I really respected, and I was completely surprised when she said, "Yes, you should absolutely do it."

As I began to work on the nomination, she came to my door one day and said she wanted to make a donation. I knew enough by that stage to say, "No, just wait until the official election campaign, and then you can have a tax receipt," but she insisted. On election night I learned she had died the day before. She had had cancer, and knew she was dying, but she wanted to support me before she went. That impacted me.

Perhaps it is part of the female experience, but community was, and is, very important to me. A few months after being elected, a close family friend died, but no one told me, and no one told me of her funeral because they figured I would be too busy in the legislature. I was devastated that anyone would assume the death of a close family friend would not be important to me. Those messages stay with me, and I determined I would never let that happen again.

I was a single parent when I was elected, and in retrospect, I think my children were just barely old enough for it to be okay for me to be running. I had a male campaign manager who talked about other 'unmanageable candidates,' and I got the message, *whatever you do, you'd better not be an unmanageable candidate.* Then I realized he had put my home address and phone number on my campaign literature without my permission. I had it changed, but you just cannot do that to anyone without permission. This is a big deal, especially for a single mother with two young teenage daughters who were sometimes home alone.

I also did not know it was unusual to be sent out campaigning by myself, and there were unnerving comments that might not have been made to a male candidate. In fact, there were many, many things that quite frankly might not have been said to a man. But people also came to me about things and talked to me about things which they might not have discussed with a man; I don't know. I still swear I had one of the most interesting constituencies to represent, and I am glad I was always known as a constituency politician.

I discovered immediately, though, after I was elected, that there was great effort to make the MLAs relationship to constituents subordinate to the relationship to caucus. One of the big things I was missing, and still am missing, is not having a background in team sports. Many of the men in the legislature had played football or hockey, and they were large, strong, imposing figures to whom people gravitated. They knew at an almost intuitive level, how to move in a group. They understood that the whole team does not rush after the ball at once, and that some people's job is to decoy and distract.

The physicality of the legislature is fascinating. The legislative chamber is very small, and the seats are almost piled on top of each other. Sometimes to avoid crossing between the Speaker and a member who is speaking, you practically have to crawl out. The male/female dynamic breaks down pretty fast in those circumstances! Sometimes the point is to exhaust people physically, while they are trying to keep the show on the road. After a while, everyone is hot and sweaty, and their eyes are burning after hours and hours of filibustering. Endurance is important; I remember watching Maureen MacDonald stand for six hours straight to defend a budget as the Minister of Health. I admire that kind of durability.

My advice would be to never, ever stand for office just because you want to be in office; you must have a purpose. Do not do it unless you have something you really believe needs to be done. Realize too, that you are not engaging in a career. I have always regarded elected office as fulfilling a contract. If you are elected, you have been selected to perform a contract to represent the people of the constituency and the members of the party within the legislature. That is it. Full stop. No one is entitled to do that forever.

22. The HONOURABLE DIANA WHALEN
LIBERAL MLA FOR CLAYTON PARK WEST (PREVIOUSLY HALIFAX CLAYTON PARK)
2003–2017
First Female Deputy Premier
Minister of Finance & Treasury Board
Minister of Justice & Attorney General
Halifax Regional Councillor District 16 2000–2003

It is hard to say exactly what led me to run for office. I decided to put my name on the municipal ballot in 2000, after being very involved as a volunteer in the brand new neighbourhood of Clayton Park West in Halifax. I had moved into the area when it was literally being carved out of the woods. My children were small and I got involved in the new neighbourhood association, my church, and then the elementary school. There were issues to address—we needed playgrounds, crosswalks, traffic lights and, after a few years, we needed a new school. I learned a lot by being involved in these various challenges and I wanted to have a greater say in how the community grew.

Running for office was not something that I had thought of growing up. My career start was unconventional as my husband became a diplomat and we moved to South Korea, and later Australia, and Jamaica. I learned to adapt to new situations and found work opportunities as a management consultant. I saw firsthand that there were different ways to do things in each place I lived. As my family settled back in Halifax and I got involved in the community, I wanted to bring some of these different approaches to the Halifax Regional Council. It was daunting to take that step and I could not have done it without help from family, friends, and mentors.

From my first days in politics, women were few in number and, at times, overlooked or not taken seriously. Although there were only six women out of twenty-four councillors on the HRM Council, I saw how effective and prepared the women were. It was important for us to stand up and be counted. Sadly, there are only two women out of sixteen councillors in 2020.[8]

After three years on city council, I decided to run for MLA in Halifax Clayton Park. In that election, all three major parties nominated a female candidate and this was a first for the province. I won and found I was the only woman in the twelve-member Liberal caucus. It was a very masculine environment. Prior to the election there had been no women at all in the caucus. I had to get used to sport analogies like, 'keep your elbows up,' 'get them in the corner,' and 'rag the puck.' It was such a cultural shift for me. To be heard, I had to be determined and persistent.

In the absence of women colleagues, there was often little support for the policies that I was proposing. The idea of a February holiday is a perfect example. Beginning in 2005, I championed this policy, and raised it year after year in the face of considerable resistance. The idea was brought to my attention by a woman who had lived in Alberta and really appreciated their 'Family Day.' As I looked into it, I agreed and was further motivated by my understanding of the pressure that families are under. Often my own caucus had disagreements about it and at times, I was criticized for proposing this holiday. Business groups objected to the idea every time it came up and that split the support in our caucus. Finally, a poll question about a winter holiday showed that over 80 percent of Nova Scotians were supportive and women were even more in favour of this idea. A bill was finally passed under Premier McNeil and we celebrated the first Nova Scotia Heritage Day in 2015.

In 2007, I ran for the Liberal leadership. This was my most ambitious campaign, taking me out of Clayton Park West to campaign across the province in rural areas and towns far from Halifax. We were successful in building strong support thanks to the amazing people who worked so hard and believed in me. I came close, winning 47.5 percent of the votes with support from ridings across the province.

Although I was disappointed, I know that I have helped pave the way for other women to run in future leadership races. I take pride in being the woman who has come closest to the premier's office in Nova Scotia and I know that one day we will see a woman as our premier. Was gender a factor in the leadership race? It is hard to say but as it became clear that I had a shot at winning, some people started to say (even to my supporters) that the province was not ready for a woman premier. At the time only one woman had been elected premier of a Canadian province and that was Rita Johnston in British Columbia in 1991.

It was hard trying to position myself as a woman who could be premier and as a person who had the substance and gravitas needed. The positioning of a woman candidate requires a lot of thought. While you may not want to be 'the woman candidate' and play on only one dimension of your leadership, at the same time, others will be considering it consciously or unconsciously. I wanted to demonstrate

---

[8] Prior to the submission of this book, Halifax Regional Council achieved gender parity for the first time in history. Eight women, including former MLA, Becky Kent, were elected on October 17, 2020.

that I had the right background and knowledge to be the leader of the Liberal Party. I knew that my experience and education stacked up strongly against the other three candidates and I had proven I was electable as MLA. I discovered there are a lot of factors at play for the votes of party delegates. The leadership campaign took a lot of courage but I have no regrets.

It is a good feeling to know that I am thought of as a trailblazer in the legislature. I was honoured to be asked by Premier McNeil to be the deputy premier in 2013, the first woman to hold that position. At the same time, I became the Minister of Finance which fit well with my education and work experience. I chaired the Treasury and Policy Board which controls government spending. When I was the Minister of Justice, we appointed more diverse candidates and women to the bench and I was able to expand restorative justice significantly.

Justice offered the opportunity to influence individual practices and the culture within the Justice Department. I worked with the First Nations community in Wagmatcook to plan the opening of the first wellness court to serve their community and with the chief justice to co-chair the Access to Justice Committee that looked for ways to overcome barriers to justice such as poverty and racism. I am also very proud of the ambitious Accessibility Act, my last piece of legislation passed in 2017.

While I accomplished a lot as a cabinet minister, one can also be effective in opposition where I sat for ten years. For example, while in opposition in 2004, I introduced a bill to require booster seats for children up to nine years of age. I wanted us to take action before there was a major accident. I must have been persuasive as the government agreed to pass my bill. Of course, it does not always work that way as I found when I introduced the Domestic Violence Elimination Act in 2008. It had a lot of support from women's organizations and went through second reading and law amendments. Sadly, at the last minute, the Minister of Justice did not call the bill for third reading and it was never passed. Women's groups were outraged.

When I reflect on my fourteen years in the legislature, I am particularly proud of the preservation of 4,000 acres of urban wilderness known as the Blue Mountain Birch Cove Lakes (BMBCL) Wilderness Area. I worked with a core group of knowledgeable advocates and introduced a bill to include the BMBCL in the Wilderness Protection Act. We held events, spoke at many meetings and raised public support. In 2009, the government protected the area that is bounded by Clayton Park West, Timberlea, and Hammonds Plains. The Liberal government has since added to it and it is now one of the largest urban wilderness areas in Canada.

While I no longer hold elected office, I continue to work as co-chair of the Friends of BMBCL. This is an amazing group of volunteers that are advocating to see the area enlarged to become a regional park as promised in Halifax's Regional Plan. That will finally make this beautiful area more open to the public and will complete the work I started in the legislature.

I left politics with a fairly positive view of the whole process. I spent a total of seventeen years in public service. I have been in the centre of some controversies, especially in my role as Minister of Finance at a time when we were determined to control spending and set the province on a stronger financial path. I certainly felt the weight of being in government. Every decision has its impact and no matter how you look at it, there are always some people in favour and some who are critical. The difficulties were balanced by the satisfaction of making a contribution and I experienced that both in opposition and while serving in the cabinet.

I would encourage young women to put their names on a ballot. It doesn't have to be at the provincial level. There is a lot to learn and contribute to at all levels of civic engagement. Being active in an organization or a community group, you learn a lot about the people who are making decisions that affect you. When I got involved locally, I didn't realize that it was a first step in my political life.

I believe that most people, men and women alike, go into politics to make a difference and to do something positive for their communities. That was certainly my motivation and I am proud of my work on behalf of my constituents, as an MLA, as a cabinet minister and as deputy premier of Nova Scotia.

23. The HONOURABLE CAROLYN BOLIVAR GETSON
PC MLA FOR LUNENBURG WEST 2003–2009
Minister of Natural Resources
Minister of Seniors, and Emergency Management
Minister of Immigration
Minister of Environment and Labour
Minister of Human Resources
Minister responsible for the Public Service Commission and Advisory Council on the Status of Women
Councillor in the Municipality of Lunenburg 1997–2003
Mayor of the Municipality of Lunenburg 2016–Present

I had an interest in politics that I can trace back to my childhood and the conversations around my family's kitchen table. I come from a politically split family—my dad was a Liberal, and my mom was a Conservative. Election time was always a controversial time in the house, because each parent would go dutifully cancel the other's vote. Politics was a frequent topic of conversation, and from a very early age I was taken along to political events.

My first foray into politics was participating in student council in high school. I attended several political picnics and I recall one where John Diefenbaker flew in by helicopter to a field in Pinehurst for the annual Tory Picnic and gave an inspiring address. I also helped with many campaigns and was always there on election day to get the vote out for many elections.

In 1997, I decided to run for municipal council with the Municipality of the District of Lunenburg. I was a small business owner, and I knew a lot of people personally in my community. My brother came home one night and said, "You know 'so and so' is not going to vote for you." I asked, "He's not? Why wouldn't he vote for me?" He replied, "He won't vote for a woman."

I was floored. It never crossed my mind that people in the late '90s might feel that way. I went to see this individual, and he told me that he did not feel that women should be running for politics, that it was not our place.

When I ran for re-election four years later, I went back to his house and he apologized. He told me that I proved that he was wrong about women in politics. It was a step in the right direction, but it really set me back to hear that. And even now, more than two decades later, I still come across that attitude. People may not come out and say it anymore, but you know it. Those feelings are still there.

Near the end of my second term, I decided to run provincially. I had always planned to make the leap to provincial politics and felt my experience in municipal government had prepared me for the move. I was elected as MLA in 2003. I went into the legislature as the only female cabinet minister and only female in the Progressive Conservative caucus at that time.

Sitting in the legislature, I was surrounded by an excellent group of individuals. Instead of being concerned that I would not have a voice, I felt listened to more than most because I was a woman. I remember one time in cabinet we were discussing a proposal I felt strongly about. I said, "I can't support that." In cabinet, we ruled by consensus. The premier pointed at me and two ministers and said, "You three leave the room and come back when you have a decision that she can support."

I commend the Premier for recognizing the importance of this subject to me and asking others to help with a resolution. Even so, being the only woman in my caucus was a lonely spot to be in. I am glad to see that we now have sixteen women in the legislature. During my tenure, there were women in the other caucuses, and we got together. It became a peer group where we could find encouragement, and usually leave the political side out of it. It is important to have that support.

When I was first elected to council in 1997, I had three children under the age of four. That was a first for my council. When I was appointed to cabinet, I was one of the first female cabinet ministers to ever have young children. Policies to allow women to take their children with them to work didn't exist at that time. It never would have been possible without my parents, my husband, and my husband's parents. It is a family affair when you set out to run for politics. It changes a lot, and you miss a lot.

I ran three times as MLA, but I was defeated in 2009 when the NDP won the government. I came back and ran municipally in 2011 and won a council seat again. In 2016, I ran for mayor. The knowledge I acquired over the years in my many roles has been very beneficial, and something I take into this role as mayor. The contacts that I have made throughout municipal and provincial politics are invaluable. It is not something you can learn from a book.

One accomplishment I am particularly proud of is the campaign school for women. In the fall of 2003, as a newly elected MLA, I attended a campaign school at the University of British Columbia. I returned home intending to start a campaign school for women in Nova Scotia. I was the Minister responsible for the Advisory Council on the Status of Women at the time. We quickly developed a campaign school through a partnership between Mount Saint Vincent University and the Advisory Council on the Status of Women, and it was a great success. I am proud to say it has continued in some format ever since. It includes everything from door knocking modules, to how to fundraise, to why you want to run, and what you should be doing leading up to an election campaign. It really takes women through the whole process of what is involved in becoming an elected official.

During the very first campaign school in Nova Scotia, I was slated to give the keynote address. My twelve-year-old daughter was listening to me rehearse my speech. I was going over some of the barriers and the reasons why women do not run, and she looked at me and asked, "Mommy, why wouldn't they vote for a woman?" Hearing that was powerful. The next generation of women coming through elected office are going to be that much more ready for the challenge of leadership.

One of the barriers women still face is the ability to fundraise. Men can fundraise for political life easier than women. That has always been the case. When you run municipally, that fundraising job is really yours to do. It does hinder a lot of individuals from being able to step forward. While there are grants available from organizations to help women run for elected office, it is still very expensive. If you are employed, you need to have the ability to take leave from work and be able to return to your job if you are not elected. These are all considerations and barriers to running.

When I started, I was told that you have to have thick skin to be a politician. Nothing has changed. There will be days you want to run the other way. When people are passionate about an issue, you need a very thick skin to handle some of the things they might say to you. But it is vitally important as a politician that you stay in dialogue with your constituents, that you call them back and follow up with them.

In 1997, I was the youngest person on our municipal council, and I am still the youngest person on my municipal council in 2020. I really hope to see more young people run for office. I think in public office, we need to be reflective of the population we serve—and we really are not. Diversity is good in any organization, so it would be nice to see that diversity throughout our political institutions. That is how you hear from all perspectives. Sitting in cabinet and listening to the Minister of Community Services speak about childcare, I would find myself thinking, *No that's not right. That isn't what we need to do. You have a different perspective.* There are topics where women have different perspectives than men. And probably vice versa. But you need everyone around the table for that reason—for constructive debate, and for the best decision making.

Right now, we are making decisions for the generations coming behind us, and I want to make sure they are going to be reflective of that generation. The best way to do that is to have those people at the table. That is where we will see change.

Photo courtesy of Judy Streatch

24. The HONOURABLE JUDY STREATCH
PC MLA FOR CHESTER-ST. MARGARET'S 2005–2009
Minister of Tourism, Culture and Heritage
Minister of Community Services
Minister of Communications Nova Scotia
Minister of Education

I was born into a family that believed in public service as part of our fibre. It was part of who we were. I lived in a community in rural Nova Scotia, and politics was very much a part of the fabric of our life. I come from a family of politicians. My father, Kenny Streatch, was a politician who served in the provincial government of John Buchanan for fifteen years. My husband, Gerald Keddy, was a member of Parliament for eighteen years. My brother, Steve Streatch, serves in municipal council in Halifax. Something that I have always been very proud of as far as my political tenure is that my father and I are the one of the only father/daughter combinations to have ever sat in the provincial legislature. I am sure that there are fathers and sons that we would recognize, but a father and daughter pair is a little bit different.

    Aside from my time in politics, my other profession is being an educator. I have always believed that being an educator, teacher, and principal is in itself a public service. I had moved my family to the

South Shore and was working in education there. After the passing of our MLA John Chataway, there was an opportunity to run in a by-election in Chester-St. Margaret's. I was ready at the time and I had established myself as a community member in the area. I belonged to the Progressive Conservative Party for fundamental personal reasons. I still believe in the philosophy, the reasoning, and the background of the Progressive Conservative movement. I sought the nomination, and then went on to win the by-election in 2005. I also won in the 2006 general election after that. In 2009, our government fell, and I was not re-elected for a third term.

When I was elected, there were only three women in our party—Carolyn Bolivar-Getson, Karen Casey, and myself. We all had different personalities. We were all different in the way we approached things. I enjoyed being outspoken. I enjoyed having a very loud and commanding voice. It was never easy to dismiss me. I had a natural presence, which perhaps made it a bit easier for me to exist in a man's political world.

Having said that, it was also a challenge. There is no question that being a woman in government and being a woman in politics was, and still is, different. I cannot imagine anyone calling my father, or my husband, or my male colleagues, and complaining about their outfit. I had those calls. It floored me the first time it happened. I thought, *Is this really what matters? The colour of my outfit?* I remember one day my constituency assistant had an email about the way I was wearing my hair. There were situations when people would question things about me as a woman that they would not question a man about.

I remember when I was first elected, we were in the legislature and one of the opposition members used the word 'fluff' to me. He said, "That was a fluffy answer." Well, I flew into a fit. I said, "You can't say that my answers are fluff, and you can't say that I don't know what I'm talking about just because I'm a woman." I think it sort of set him back. He said, "I didn't mean that, Judy. I didn't mean that. It was something that was not meant to offend you." I said, "Well, would you call one of your male colleagues *fluff*?" And he admitted that he wouldn't.

The things that I took away from politics that are the most meaningful to me are the people I met and the opportunities to effect positive change in their lives. Those were the things that were most important to me. I had a very challenging portfolio. In the beginning of my career, I was responsible for Community Services, which is an extremely difficult, complicated, and fragile portfolio. It deals with the most vulnerable and challenging sectors of government. I met some of the most honest, real, and true men and women during that time. The folks who were the most vulnerable and the most at need gave me the opportunity to help them, and that truly was an honour for me.

The project and initiative that I was most proud of our government for was the creation of the SchoolsPlus program.[9] Being back in the classroom and back in the school environment now, I see the daily benefits of having the SchoolsPlus program in our schools. When our government brought that program in, we recognized that we had children who were falling through the cracks and getting lost, and parents did not know where to turn. Our vision was for those families to have an opportunity to liaise with a coordinator at the school on a neutral ground, and the individual would be able to help

---

[9] SchoolsPlus is a strategy to improve coordination and collaboration in delivery of programs and services for youth.

those families build relationships and bridge those gaps. I see that every day. I see what it means on the ground in my own school. I know that it was the right thing to do.

If you have got the fire in your belly, if you believe in the cause, if you can find a group of individuals that you can connect with, run. Do not wait. Timing is everything in politics, but do not be scared and do not be hesitant. Surround yourself with positive people who believe in the same things as you do. Know that you are doing it for the right reasons—do not do it because you think that it is glorious. Do not do it because you think it is a great salary. Do not do it because you think it will look good on a resume. Do it because you know that it is the right thing for you to do. Do not be afraid that because you are a woman you will not be taken seriously or you will not be able to achieve your goals, because you can.

Serving our community makes us stronger, makes our families stronger, and in this day and age, I think we need to go back to that core. I think that service needs to be a part of a lot of families' core base. Politics right now is very toxic. I managed to get out before social media really became an everyday, non-stop part of political life. We need good people in office. We need honest and solid people. I think a lot of times, people shy away from politics because it can be so toxic, and that worries me. The foundation of our political system is such that it relies on having good, quality candidates from all walks of life. We need everybody around that table to really make the system work.

The other piece that is part of my story is the fact that I had a very large family. I have six children—four biological children and two children that came to me through my marriage to Gerald. We raised a family of six in the community that was extremely supportive. Our families were very supportive. It was never just *my* foray into politics, or *my* time, or 'Judy Streatch' as the politician—it was all of us as a family. My children sacrificed a lot so that I could achieve and follow my dreams.

When I was not re-elected, they were my foundation. It was not easy to step back into the life that I had set aside to go into politics, but they made it possible. My story really is my own, but it cannot be separated from my children, my husband, my extended family, and my community. I would not be able to do what I did without all of them and I know that a big part of who I am is thanks to them. I see them all grown and living their own lives, and I know that what we lived through as a family made them stronger. It was not always easy. My heart is heavy a lot of times because of what the children had to go through. But again, it was part of my core to serve my community and I know my children served their community. That is where I come from. That is who we are. That would be our story.

Photograph by Mosy Photography

25. The HONOURABLE KAREN CASEY
LIBERAL MLA FOR COLCHESTER NORTH 2006–PRESENT
Deputy Premier
Minister of Finance & Chair of Finance and Treasury Board
Minister of Education
Minister of Health

I am an educator. I had about sixteen years of experience teaching in the classroom before I moved into administration for another fourteen years. That gave me a total of thirty years working in public education in a variety of capacities. I found teaching to be extremely rewarding. When you are working with young kids, there is a concept, there is a skill, or there is a bit of information that you want them to have. Your challenge is—how do you impart that into them so that they learn? I quite enjoyed that, and the reward is often immediate and very exciting for the teacher and the child.

I retired from education, and I still wanted to do something that I felt was using the skill set that I had. That skillset was helping solve problems and bring resolution to some issues that average Nova Scotians have. In 2006, the opportunity came at election time for candidates to put their name forward. I was ready to do that. I had retired and formed a consulting firm, and while that was working fine, it just was not giving me that satisfaction I thought I would get. I sought the nomination, I won the nomination, and then I went into the election and I won that.

As an MLA, you provide that opportunity for your constituents to come in and share their concerns with you. You work with them to try to bring resolution. I am into my thirteenth year at this, but I still find it very rewarding. It is the same skill set you use as a teacher. It is very rewarding when you can bring resolution to an issue that a constituent might have.

As a teacher, I was working with both male and female teachers. When I went on to be an assistant superintendent, I did go into a male-dominated environment. There had never been a female assistant superintendent on that particular board. There were five assistant superintendents, four of them were men and I was the only woman. That brought me around a decision-making table with men. I never felt that my voice was not heard. I think that you have to establish credibility with the team you are with, and I was able to do that. Many of them had seen me come through the ranks and knew I was capable, so I had that credibility. But it was most certainly a male-dominated table of decision makers.

I think you need to know your subject, you need to think before you speak, you need to do your research before you come out, and then when you come out with a strong knowledge-base and you are able to articulate that well, people pay attention. I pride myself in doing my homework before I make a statement, introduce legislation, or whenever I go before the media or public. I like to make sure I am as ready as I possibly can be, because I think that is where you build credibility and that is when people look at you and listen to what you are saying. You have to be confident in yourself—not overly confident, but confident. That will get you the respect and make people pay attention because they respect your opinion and they respect you as a person.

Provincially we have done a lot of things since I was elected with Stephen McNeil in 2013. We have made a lot of difference. The population in the province is the highest it has ever been. Unemployment is low, employment is high. There is lots of private sector investing and job creation. I said one time, "I hope I live to see the population of Nova Scotia get to be one million." Well, it's up to 970,000 now. I think being part of that, and seeing that you are making lives better for average Nova Scotians, is encouraging me to stay on and to continue.

But really, my pride is in the fact that I touched so many lives as a public school teacher. Thousands of kids would have gone through my classrooms, or I would have been their principal when they were in school. You know that in some small way, you have made their life better. Some of them come back and tell you that. You know inside, and that is where that reward comes both for you and for the learner. When somebody grasps an idea, it is very rewarding. I pride myself in the fact that in some way, I have made a difference for a lot of people.

I never forget where I came from. As a rural MLA, I grew up in the country, my constituents live in the country. I understand a lot of their issues and concerns, and they know I do because they know where I came from. They are comfortable and confident that I understand and I will help. Do not be afraid to let people know who you are, where you came from, what you stand for, and that will get you the respect you need to go on.

26. VICKI CONRAD
NDP MLA FOR QUEENS 2006–2013

I have had a lot of very diverse jobs over the years, and I have always had a political edge from a very early age. Politics was a big deal in our family. During elections, issues and candidates were discussed. As I got closer to voting age, it was clear I had a different set of political views than much of my family—I would have been the first NDP voter. When I was in high school, I ran for student council and sat for a one-year term in grade ten. I was very involved in a number of social clubs. I have always been aware of injustices and problems that I felt I could help change for the better. Over the years I would write letters to speak out for or against certain issues—I remember returning a postcard with a written response to Prime Minister Pierre Trudeau regarding a particular bird at that time being identified as a species at risk. I would often approach teachers in school about making certain changes or to identify specific issues. I often stood as a lone rebel or in solidarity with other students for causes we felt important to us. I was always drawn to representing other people and representing the underdog.

Over the years, I worked on the front lines in long-term care homes, home care, and worked as a residential counsellor supporting people with special needs living in group homes. I ran my own businesses, and my husband and I have run a small diverse farm for over thirty years. Regardless of my jobs and positions, I was always engaged in my community and held volunteer positions on various committees and local organizations. I was interested in hearing what people on the ground were experiencing. I worked hard and people could trust me to do what I said I was going to do, whether it was advocating on their behalf, or researching the facts and filling out the required paperwork to get things done.

During my time in home care, I was instrumental in organizing the first union for home support workers in Queens County, and after leading workers to go out on strike, we successfully negotiated a number of contracts that saw better wages and conditions for workers on the frontlines—who were mostly women. It was that experience that gave me my first glimpse into the world of politics. I excelled at meeting with negotiators, employers, and cabinet ministers and got very good at negotiating and advocating for the needs of others. I was always putting my hand up to help make change.

In the '90s, I worked on a few election campaigns for the NDP. The party's policies aligned with a lot of my values, and I loved the excitement of the elections. In 2000 I ran for municipal council in Queens County, and in 2003 Darrell Dexter asked me if I would run provincially. Knowing that he had faith in my ability to be a leader in the community and to win the seat sealed the deal for me. I was the first NDP and first woman candidate to ever be elected in Queens, after fifty-three years of having a Conservative representative.

I have always been self-confident, and aggressively put my voice out there when it was needed. I was not intimidated by being a woman in politics, but I realized very quickly that politics, even today, is still very much a man's world. It is hard to break through and be heard on what your beliefs are, how you think policy should be structured, and what changes you think are needed within government.

When I was first elected in 2006, I was naive. I remember my first day sitting at the caucus table, my blinders were ripped off immediately to the reality of politics. Staffers and seasoned members reinforced for us newbies that the next campaign started the day we were elected, and the job we needed to concentrate on most was getting ourselves re-elected. Of course, we were also told to work hard on behalf of our constituents. But what I was hearing was that my job really was about being re-elected.

There was such a difference between working in my constituency and working around the tables in Halifax. I was constantly juggling those two very different worlds. Some of my proudest moments were in the constituency office, and the people who worked for me did an amazing job. Over time, I realized that my assistant was actually doing most of the work that I really wanted to do myself; the hands-on work with individual constituents. It is easy to lose touch with your home base when you are in the world of politics in the city. There is lobbying by department staff, corporate entities, and by members. There is jockeying, the constant political bantering, deal-making, and trading of information usually around a few drinks. There is a certain excitement in the political world and it is easy to get caught up in the perceived grandiose of it all. I believe it was John Holm who once said to me, "Everyone knows you when you are a politician, when you're done everyone forgets your name."

One of my most satisfying moments was helping an elderly couple who did not have a working washroom, and no running water. They had fallen through the cracks of the system for years and had never been able to make any headway in getting the assistance they needed. Helping to lift that family out of that situation was important to me. We do not often talk about the individuals that we actually help in this job, because it is not as glamorous as building a school or investments in highway construction.

The people that elect you really do believe that you can make a difference. To a certain degree that is true, especially on an individual level. However, the really big issues such as biomass or fish farms get bogged down in lobbying and regulations. Citizen engagement through public consultation is about soothing the disgruntled voices. Every current government is dealing with remnants of the same issues of the previous government. We were dealing with issues that the Conservative government before us was dealing with—in a lot of ways, nothing really changes and the day to day work of each government usually looks the same, just a different name on the door and letterhead. Take away the party stripe, the colour, and government wheels still turn ever so slowly. They make the same mistakes, bail out the same corporate entities, go head to toe with the unions, and pave lots of roads before election time.

I still believe the NDP government could have implemented a lot of progressive policies over time had they been given a second term, and there is no question that we stepped up on a number of issues. When Bowater Mersey announced its pending closure, it was indeed progressive and the right thing to do to secure the hard-earned pensions for the many workers who would be out of work. Too, the creation of the economic transition team allowed many stakeholders from the region to develop a new path forward after Bowater. But overall, I feel we lost sight of what was most important to folks, and I believe we squandered so much opportunity. I was disappointed at how difficult it was becoming to express my voice. I was appointed as caucus chair, which at times felt like a token position where I could not weigh in with my opinion in quite the same way as other members.

I loved meeting with constituents. I was never good at remembering names, but I never forgot a face. During a campaign your time is limited on the doorsteps, you hear of the immediate things that are a constant visual (like potholes) or you get a lot of commentary on the promises each party is messaging and each candidate spouts out like a mantra. Campaigns are driven on hot button issues that will get people riled up. The political party machines are constantly taking the pulse of the electorate and creating the message, and then the candidate on the doorstep reinforces the message. When I first ran in 2003, the campaign platform revolved on the issue of public auto insurance. I took petitions around to every corner store, every gas station, and we had thousands of signatures from across the province. They knew with insurance rates going up and affecting the pockets book of every car owner, they had a hot button issue. But when we formed the government, we did not do it. But it was a great campaign, a great message, and it got people riled up. At that moment, as an elected voice, I started to feel very ingenuine.

I was very loyal to the party, to the premier, and to my colleagues. You have to be loyal to your party to forward the policies you believe in. But over time that loyalty gets a little jaded. Especially when you realize that the circle of power is very small, and you only have the illusion of being on the inside. There were many times I started to feel at odds with toeing the party line, and I knew other caucus members were struggling too. When I was in opposition, I stood up on my feet over and over again voicing concern over the growth of fish farms in Queens. I was encouraged by my colleagues to do so. I was down on the beaches with Darrell Dexter and a megaphone. I passionately believed that we, as an NDP Government, would point the way to offering better solutions to growing the rural economy. When we formed government, we turned around and invested $25 million into Cooke Aquaculture. I was not even asked to sit at that decision-making table. I learned of the investment announcement literally minutes before I was to start a caucus meeting at a retreat in Shelburne. Later, I had to carry that message of investment back to my constituents who believed in me and our government. I was not given, in my estimation today, the respect to know of these developments beforehand, maybe because they thought I would have dug in my heels and my rebel streak would have revealed itself. I felt betrayed and disheartened and started to realize there were too many times I was feeling my voice being stifled. And I had to say, *Okay. I am no longer where I want to be.*

I have reflected a lot on the seven years I was an elected voice, I have taken time to think about where I was, being both on the opposition benches and then sitting in government. I have reflected on how it affected me, how I changed. Are my values different today than when I went in?

For me, I know I lost the confidence to stand up and say to the premier and to the Minister of Fisheries how I felt. Looking back, it was not so much that the investment was made, rather it was the fact that I was not invited to at least be part of the conversation around that issue. Maybe this is what happens to some of us women. It was not the first time I doubted myself or felt my confidence erode. That was a gradual process, and I became increasingly disappointed in how dysfunctional the political world really is.

We absolutely do need young people and young women running for public office. I do not have all of the answers, but there needs to be more thinking outside of the box. We do not need to do things the way they always have been done. It is about thinking outside of those old ideas, whether it is on the campaign trail or sitting around the boardroom tables. **It is important that you know yourself well and not forget who you were and where you came from before entering the political arena**. It can be exhilarating and exciting, it can be a lot of obnoxious personalities, swaggering egos and pomp and ceremony. It can be fun, and it can feel like you are playing with power. You have to remember why you are there.

When I decided not to reoffer, I wanted to remain loyal and I missed the opportunity to share the real truth about why I was leaving. It was not because I was looking to do something else, it was because I felt deflated, disappointed, and I no longer had the passion. I could not in good faith just hang on to my seat because I was able to. When I made public my decision not to reoffer, two male members from different sides of the house actually suggested to me, "Vicki, you are crazy not to reoffer, you know you can win the Queens seat hands down and probably keep it for as long as you want…think of the years of pension you can build up." Those phrases, absolutely, without a doubt, reaffirmed for me that I was making the right decision. I had gone from 'Vicki' to 'Vicki Conrad, MLA,' and after seven years I really needed to get back and find out who Vicki was.

Some days I still ponder all of this. Why did I allow my voice to be squashed? Was it because it was an environment of mostly men? Was it something else? I think as a woman, you need to be clear about who you are, and get ready to go toe-to-toe if you have to, especially for the constituents who elect you. I think all people who put their name on a ballot do so for the right reasons, but over time things change. People get comfortable and can lose sight of why they are sitting in the seats they are—it should always be about the constituents.

All in all, you can always cut through the reeds and untangle some of the good that governments can be capable of.

27. BECKY KENT
NDP MLA FOR COLE HARBOUR-EASTERN PASSAGE 2007–2013
Councillor in the Halifax Regional Municipality for District 8, Woodside and Eastern Passage 2004-2007
Councillor in the Halifax Regional Municipality for District 3, Dartmouth South-Eastern Passage 2020–Present

I grew up in the rural community of Shelburne, Nova Scotia. It is a lot like Eastern Passage, where I live now and raised my children. After graduating university, I started a career with Nova Scotia Power, but left to raise my children. I was an active community participant, often in leadership roles, and I came up with ideas and rallied everybody together to get the job done when needed. I was taught to give back to your community so that is what was natural for me. At different times, I was approached to consider offering for political life, one of which was for municipal councillor. That is where I started, in 2004 at Halifax Regional Council as the representative for District Eight, Woodside and Eastern Passage.

The first two approaches to run were at moments in my life that would have been negatively impacted by this endeavour. My kids were young, and I was in the middle changes in our family dynamics. The third time that I was asked to consider politics my heart kind of skipped a beat. That is what I can remember the most. I thought, *I think this is the right time!* I could feel it. Long story short, I decided to run for council. I was the only woman running against four men. I had hot pink signs—I mean *fuchsia* hot pink. I defeated the incumbent of twenty-two years by about 1,500 votes—I guess people were ready for change and ready for a woman to represent them. Three years after my election to council, our local MLA had decided he was retiring and moving onto something else. He asked me if I would consider running at the provincial level. I was elected to the Nova Scotia Legislature in a by-election and served as MLA for more than six years. I spent over nine years as an elected official. I am proud of that and honoured to have had the opportunity.

People say that sometimes one has a calling to a certain type of career or vocation. I really do feel that community leadership through politics is what I am meant to do. I am a community advocate. I naturally champion for things. I want people to do well. I want people to succeed, and communities to succeed. Since leaving the position of MLA for Cole Harbour Eastern Passage just over seven years ago, I have worked for not-for-profits, and most recently in our family business. I made the decision about nine months ago to reoffer in an upcoming election, and I finally feel like myself again.[10] That is how I know that feeling from before was genuine. I had enough time to self-reflect on the joy of the career, and what I am most passionate about is absolutely community leadership. I loved it. I think I was well-received—I am naturally a people person. The hardest part about that work was that layer of society that, no matter who you are, what you do, how well you do, whether you have skeletons in your closet or not, if you are a politician—they do not like you. That was foreign to me.

I think the male-dominated environment presented itself in the legislature the most. It was very obvious to me. I did not find that I had as many challenges in my role with my colleagues and peers outside the legislature as I did inside. I think there is more to prove for many when a TV camera and media are present. I also believe that women do not always go to that dominant space of proving themselves by way of diminishing others. I think that in general, women speak more genuinely and I like that about myself and that I am a woman with a different approach and perspective. Don't get me wrong, this is not the case for all men and all women. In the Legislature it was more obvious to me.

When I joined the NDP, we were in the official opposition and I was a backbencher, where I had a chance to rise in the legislature and speak on a bill that was on the floor. I got up and spoke to it, and I thought I did a good job. I was well prepared through the support of the caucus and the researchers. Then, one of my male colleagues stood to speak and pretty much minimized my whole speech. He kind of undermined it. I thought to myself, *Wow, he's supposed to be on my team!*

We both finished but I was angry about the way I was undermined by a team member, so I walked right over to him and I said, "Don't ever do that to me again." He was surprised and taken aback that I challenged him and called him out. "You might want to look at the tapes. You basically undermined everything I said. Nobody is allowed to do that to me. And especially somebody on my team." I was not rude. I was assertive. I do not get ugly or mean-spirited, but I will not back down if someone is being mistreated, including myself.

He said, "Becky, I am so sorry. I did not realize." I do not think he did realize it and because of an arrogance, and this male-dominated space, it was traditionally okay to behave that way. Well, after that

---

[10] Becky won this election subsequent to this interview and was elected as Councillor for District 3. She was sworn into office on October 29, 2020.

it was like I was his best friend. He respected me and his behaviour changed completely. I think I was not seen by him until I stood up for myself. I did it responsibly, professionally, and respectfully. But I stood up to him. Not everyone has that tenacity, I know that. But it worked for me. After that we got along very well, and he was a great resource to me.

I was also deputy Speaker of the House of Assembly, which is a privilege and a great role. I loved it because I was able to be non-partisan in a partisan environment. It is a role where the Speaker of the House must insist on people being reasonable, respectful and with decorum. Not everyone wanted to do it, but I really liked that role.

From a human perspective, the thing that I feel the proudest of in relation to the work that I did is that people genuinely felt connected to me. Not every politician has that. That was brought up to me over and over again. To know that I have connected positively with the many people I encountered, I am incredibly proud of. It makes me smile. It gives me joy that I have really affected somebody in a positive way.

One significant project that I was able to accomplish in my time as MLA was when we were the NDP government. My work resulted in putting in place the funding required to create an Eastern Passage High School. That had been a thirty-five-year-long community activism issue. While it did not get built while I was an MLA, all the funding was put in place, the project was moving forward, approved, the budget was there, and the construction was en route. From a community [perspective], that was pretty exciting. Now that it is built, I can drive by the school every day and know that I played a significant role in it.

While I was on [HRM] council there was an issue related to the design and construction of the sewage treatment plant in Dartmouth. There had been a huge rift between the community, the project team, and the engineers, who often are very clinical and not necessarily community relationship builders. I had to really, really work hard to build the relationship between the municipality and the community. I feel such pride in that, because it really was the thing that was in the way of getting that project done. Once we started to rebuild [community relations], and the budget was going forward, the community's interest became more relevant at the table. I was a brand new [councillor]. Brand new. No clue about politics. No clear path to how to get it done. But I just knew that it was about people and needed to mend the relationship. In fact, one of the engineers on that project about four months after I started, said, "I owe you an apology. When you first got elected and came into the first meeting with us, all I could think was, 'Oh great, this is a stay-at-home mom who thinks that she is going to change the world and what is she going to do?' I need to apologize to you, because you have a lot to offer. You are going to do well in this job. I'm sorry I took that position." That was a very special moment for me. I felt validated, heard, seen, and recognized that as a woman, yes, formerly a stay-at-home mom, I do have a lot of perspective and skills in a role like this.

What I would say, and have said, to someone who is considering this type of journey, is this: if you are excited about politics in any part of your being, reach out to other people who have had that experience. The support you can get from other women and other people who do the job is so helpful. I have always taken the position that it did not matter what political party you supported, it did not matter if you were male or female, or whoever in your community, if you had an interest in politics, let me know and I would love to share my experiences and insight in an attempt to support your choice and process. For me, it doesn't matter where you live, if you want someone to talk about an idea or concern, give me a call. I will be happy to talk to you. I have been privileged to be in those roles, so I have an obligation to share my experience…at least I think I do.

Photo by Mosy Photography

28. The HONOURABLE KELLY REGAN
LIBERAL MLA FOR BEDFORD (PREVIOUSLY BEDFORD-BIRCH COVE) 2009–PRESENT
Minister of Labour and Advanced Education
Minister responsible for the Advisory Council on the Status of Women
Minister of Community Services

I was always interested in politics; I thought it was incredibly fascinating. Growing up, as soon as I got off the school bus at the end of the day, I would rip in the door and grab our afternoon paper. I wanted to know what was going on. But although I would read about politics—and thought it was important and fascinating—I didn't grow up with a lot of women in politics as role models. Sheila Copps was a role model—she was elected in 1981 in provincial politics. There was a woman mayor in one of the towns near where I grew up. But there really were not a lot of women in politics back then.

I went to the University of Waterloo. I have a degree in English and legal studies. I also did co-op, and my last three work terms were spent at a local television station, where we, of course, covered politics. So, I became more immersed in politics along the way. Interestingly, one of the other students I worked with at CKCO at the time was Diaene Vernile, who went on to become a cabinet minister under Premier Kathleen Wynne after hosting a television news show there for decades. We still keep in touch.

I do not think it is any surprise that I became intensely involved in politics when I began seeing Geoff Regan in the early '90s.[11] I worked on a lot of campaigns in a variety of roles, and I think different people got to know me and got to know my work. Stephen McNeil, who was then the Liberal leader but not yet premier, was asking people, "Who should run in Bedford?" and my name kept cropping up. I kept saying no because, having watched Geoff, I knew it was not a glamorous job; it is a tough job. But, after a year I finally said yes. My hesitation was very much rooted in my concern about whether I could do this job. It definitely was a confidence thing; I never anticipated that I would ever be a politician. It was not something that I thought was even possible when I was growing up. When I was younger, because so few women ran for office and were elected, I believed that if you were going to do it, you had to be some kind of superwoman. Turns out you do not.

There was an academic who spoke to a Liberal convention about a decade ago, Dr. Christine Cheng. Through her research, she discovered that ridings where women have run as candidates—even if they are not elected—are more likely to elect a woman in the future. So, even if you do not get elected, being on the ballot is valuable because it creates a path for other women in the future.

When you look at the legislature, and especially when you look at our party, there is quite a variety of different experiences and different backgrounds there. If you look at our caucus in particular, there is a diversity of experience (both personal and professional) that helps us consider more viewpoints and life experiences.

> **I like to say that we—women—are what political candidates look like. We are what politicians look like. It is not just the old, wealthy male lawyer anymore. It is all of us, with all of our lived experience.**

Stephen McNeil has noted that before I was elected, we had nine members in the Liberal caucus, and only one of those was a woman—Diana Whalen. After I came in, Stephen said the conversation changed. And then Karen Casey crossed the floor to us, and it changed more. As women became a bigger percentage of the caucus, issues of concern to women started to come forward more.

I remember, shortly after we were elected to government in 2013, the Liberal Party had an AGM luncheon, and for a change (from the usual single guest speaker), they featured all the women cabinet ministers. This was the first time Nova Scotia had five women ministers. They sat us all down and we had a little fireside chat. It was serious and funny and really highlighted all of our backgrounds and abilities. Geoff loved watching that and was so incredibly proud of all of us. And then later, Margaret Miller was added to cabinet, and we were six—once again, the most women in cabinet our province has ever had.

It is nice having a partner that I can talk to, who has been a federal cabinet minister, who knows what it is like to have to make those tough decisions. It has been helpful to me. We each understand what the other one is feeling at any given time, and I do not think a lot of couples in politics have that.

---

[11] Geoff Regan is the Member of Parliament for Halifax West. He served in the role from 1993-1997, and then from 2000-present. He was Speaker of the House of Commons from 2015-2019 and served as Minister of Fisheries and Oceans from 2003-2006.

As a result, there is a level of understanding between us, and we support each other when it is a busy time. For example, when I was running in 2017, even though Geoff was in Ottawa, he was the PIC, the 'Parent in Charge.' If the kids needed anything, that is who they called. We determined it was best not to call the parent who is on the campaign trail, you just let them do their thing. And if you are the partner who is not currently running for office, you make sure the other one has clean clothes, food to eat, and things are calm at home. It works for us.

At this point, I am most proud of some bills that we have passed on paid domestic violence leave, on maternity leave for women councillors, and by extension, for MLAs. Up until the point where I moved the resolution on the latter, MLAs had to ask the Speaker for permission to be off on any kind of leave. Not that Speaker Kevin Murphy ever would have denied it, but it made no sense to me.

I was very proud of our caucus and party when Stephen [McNeil] promised the restorative inquiry into the Home for Colored Children, and we delivered on that promise. That, and the work to ensure African Nova Scotians can get title to land their families have owned, often for centuries, was long overdue. The work that we started at Labour and Advanced Education, which Labi Kousoulis finished, to provide presumptive workers compensation coverage for first responders with PTSD—that was important too.

I am also pleased we no longer count child maintenance as income for income assistance clients, so IA clients, who are mostly single moms, have seen their monthly cheques rise an average of over $250 per month. And we have made a number of other changes that have increased the support we give to our clients.

I probably will never forget the debate in the House as all parties supported a bubble zone for women accessing abortion services. It was one of the most moving debates that I have taken part in. There was not a lot of scripted debate; we spoke from the heart. We learned so much about each other and it underlined the commonality of our experience. It was the kind of discourse I always thought we should see more of in the House.

In my personal life, I was widowed at the age of thirty, and my two eldest children are from that marriage. Back then, I was working shift work directing news programs—going to work sometimes at 4:30 in the morning. So, I was a single mom for a while before I met and married Geoff, and he adopted them. Getting through that time and raising them well…I am very proud of that. It was difficult, but they were so worth it.

29. The HONOURABLE DENISE PETERSON-RAFUSE
NDP MLA FOR CHESTER- ST. MARGARET'S 2009–2017
Minister of Community Services, responsible for Seniors and the Advisory Council on the Status of Women

---

I was always the type of person that was involved in student council, the newspaper, and other activities. I always wanted to be involved as much as I possibly could. I was very fortunate to have parents that were really supportive of that. They did not have the income level to allow me to be able to do everything, but they would always find a way to get me involved and enable me to do what was important to me. When I graduated, I took a two-year radio broadcasting course at Kingstec in Kentville. From there, I started work at a local newspaper.

A good friend of mine and I started talking and we thought, *Well maybe we should go to university.* No one in my family had ever gone to university. I did not know if I would be able to afford it. I had a male guidance counsellor in grade twelve who said, "Don't even look at filling out papers for university because you'll never make it through." That is why I went to community college in the first place. But his statement just put the bug in me. I thought, *You're not going to tell me that I can't do this.* My friend and I made a pact that we were both going to go to university. She was in the child care program at Mount Saint Vincent and I was in public relations. We actually travelled from Chester every day to keep the cost down.

After graduating, I started off in the town of Lunenburg in their Economic Development Commission. Then I started the communications department for Halifax County, and I opened my own communication business. I was doing a lot of work for non-profits such as the Canadian Living Foundation, Breakfast for Learning, the Canadian Cancer Society, the Heart and Stroke Foundation, and I thought I would like to take a try at the corporate world. I read a book that a gentleman in the Chester area wrote. I went to his house one day and said, "I read your book and I'd like to work for you." He hired me. I did work for him in the moving industry, storage businesses, and mortgages. Another important part of my life and still is today and that is volunteering. Being a volunteer enables you to help others and in addition you gain valuable experience, knowledge and friends. I received a great honour in the '90s by receiving Nova Scotia's Provincial Volunteer Award.

I got a call one day from Darrell Dexter's office. I wasn't super involved in politics at the time. I had run once to be a councillor here in Chester. There were three people in the race, and I think I came in third. I had also worked on a few campaigns for people I knew. I thought, *Why would Darrell Dexter want to talk to me?* He asked me if I had ever thought about running at the provincial level. The more he talked to me about a party that fights for those who are less fortunate, and a party that is concerned about the environment and wants to have free university education—the more I became interested. He sent a couple of MLAs out to chat with me, Marilyn More and Becky Kent. They were fascinating women to talk to. I thought, *Wow, if I could be like them, what an experience that would be. I could make a difference.* I have worked with men in a professional and a volunteer capacity where men would present an over exaggerated image of themselves as being all for equality, yet behind closed doors or one on one with you they treat you in a very chauvinistic manner. Sadly, there are rarely any paths you can take to be heard about such treatment because you know both men and women alike believe there is no basis for your concern because the man has been able to consistently present an image of supporting equalities. Unfortunately, I have also experienced dealing with women who take on personality traits of these types of men in order to try to be a part of the 'old boys' club' to succeed. However, in general I believe most women support each other and there are men who truly respect and support the talents, skills and knowledge of women without feeling threatened.

When I finally decided, I sat down with Darrell Dexter. There was one thing I wanted to know. I said, "If I am fortunate enough to win and there is a conflict between the party and what the constituents want, you may not want me Darrell, because I need to go with the community." I felt like it was the people who were hiring me. He said, "Fine with me, that's what I like." So, my journey began.

Of course, there are still barriers for women in politics. I think there is an ingrained attitude towards women that is different than towards men. I found as a woman, when you were really trying to fight hard for something that you were taking a stance on, you get a feeling that people are thinking, *Oh yeah, she's a bitch. She doesn't get along with anyone.* I would see men doing the same thing and they would say, "Oh, isn't that wonderful, he's standing his ground." The top three departments in the Darrell Dexter government were run by women, so I felt very comfortable that Darrell did see our value. But even despite that, it is a part of the whole culture of politics, and you begin to really feel the difference.

Part of that difference is from society itself and the expectations of a woman versus a man. I am very lucky because I have an extraordinarily supportive husband and 27-year-old son. If you do not have that support at home, it is a very difficult journey. There is still an attitude that needs to change.

One example is the times set for the sitting of the House. There is no looking at it through the vision of a woman and the responsibilities she has at home. I never went to a meeting where somebody said to me, "What hours in the House would be best for you?" I would look at some of the men and I knew that on the weekend going home, their house was cleaned for them, they did not have to worry about buying stuff for birthdays or stressed about Christmas because their wife or partner was getting that all together. That is changing, but I do not think we have come as far as we want to think. Political parties can say they want to get more women involved, and I believe they truly do, but we need to make the world of politics friendly for women to be able to work at the same level as the men.

Being the Minister of Community Services was very rewarding for me. At one of the conferences I went to, the children and the young adults in the care of community services started calling me 'Mama Community Services.' Out of all the accomplishments, that moment is one that I am really proud of. I always tried to make a connection with them, and the fact that that is how they saw me really made an impact. The other nickname I got was the 'huggable minister' because I love giving hugs—I even got Graham Steele to give hugs! It was quite an honour to be asked to be a minister. I had three portfolios: Community Services, Status of Women, and Seniors.

To any young woman who wants to have a fulfilling career in politics, you certainly can. Go in with your eyes open. Be who you are. Don't let anyone change you. One thing I was always told was that you have to have thick skin—but that is not who I am. Over the years as a politician, I am not afraid to say there were tears. Not in front of people, but by myself thinking, *How cruel is this?* What brought me back to reality was the people that came in my MLA office who needed help. I was able to help them, in a small or large manner. Always remember that that is what politics is about. Seeing the difference that you can actually make in people's life.

And never, ever be embarrassed to stand up when you see something that is not right. That is the hardest thing to do, because sometimes you are left standing alone.

One of the things that I have found quite frustrating after being out of politics for a while is that politics revolve around elections. It saddens me because some of the discussions we are having today are on topics we were talking about thirty to forty years ago, they just were not accomplished. Not so long ago, I heard a new MLA from one of the other parties on the radio and they said that they were frustrated that there were no housing plans in the province. When I was the minister, we developed Nova Scotia's first housing strategy. For me to continuously hear people say we have no plan is frustrating. We do have a plan. But when a new political party gets in, it seems to be the trend that you just throw out all that work. You do not want to attach your name to something that was done by another party. How ridiculous is that? Most of the time the general public does not know where it came from in the first place. I believe it is time we start acting like adults and make some real change.

There were a number of things in my life that ultimately brought me to politics. If you want to be happy in politics, you really have to know that you are doing work for good outcomes. You start off being naive and thinking you are a super-person. I made a pact with myself that I would not promise anything except that I would work the hardest I can. At the end of the day, that is what you are there for.

30. The HONOURABLE RAMONA JENNEX
NDP MLA FOR KINGS SOUTH 2009–2013
Minister of Service Nova Scotia and Municipal Relations, Emergency Management, and Immigration
Minister of Education and Early Childhood Development and Youth

I always knew I wanted to be a teacher. After high school, I went to Acadia University in Wolfville. I started my academic journey in music, then a BA with a focus on theatre arts and then I took my bachelor of education (special education). I was always involved with activities happening in high school, and many activities in university. I would speak up (to the best of my ability at the time) on social justice issues.

When my children were very young, my friend, Jacquie de Mestral, asked me to work on her NDP campaign. She was running for MLA in Kings West. Jacquie and I had met while serving together on a board and developed a friendship. From that point on, I was involved with the New Democratic Party as an active volunteer. I have held a number of positions in two constituencies and at the provincial level. I worked on approximately sixteen campaigns, usually in the role of campaign manager. As part of the provincial nomination committee, I was always on the lookout for people with skills and passion. I looked at them through the lens of being a good voice for Nova Scotia. In 2009, Darrell Dexter asked, "Has anyone ever asked you to run?" I said, "No. No one has ever asked me to run." He was surprised and then asked if I would put my name forward. I told him I needed to speak to my family first. I spoke with my four children and my youngest son said, "You should have done it years ago, Mom." Because I was asked, I put my name forward for nomination and I was very happy to earn the voters' confidence in Kings South and have the honour of being the MLA.

The reason I ran was because I was asked. If you do not ask, the seed does not get planted. I know that Alexa McDonough was a champion for asking and inviting people to engage in politics. The most important thing about involving people, especially women, is making sure they are asked. Many people will not step forward unless they are asked even if they might be thinking about it. I was asked by Jacquie to work on her campaign and that is how I got involved. I asked a lot of people to work on campaigns and also to run. You build your community by asking and inviting people to participate.

I have been invited by schools, university classes, and organizations to speak about my experiences as a woman in politics and I have always minimized anything negative that happened while I was an elected member. I think all female Ministers and MLAs have stories about people deferring to their male assistants or assuming they were the 'wife' and being overlooked at functions and events. Overall, my experience as a cabinet minister and as a MLA within the legislature was positive and rewarding. When you are in the House, there's a general respect for the person from all members. I always conducted myself with appropriate decorum, never heckling. I was disappointed to be the target of vitriol from some members in opposition during debate and question period. Some members took politics personally and made things uncomfortable for me. I feel one does not need to engage in rude behaviour as it turns people off of politics, undermines the work of government and does not set a good example for our youth. There are many people who I served with in the legislature that I consider to be friends who are not from the party that I represented. Most people run for office because they want to do the best for their community and for Nova Scotia.

Over the years I have heard boys say, "When I grow up, I'm going to be prime minister." But I did not hear the same from girls. It has not been my experience to hear girls or young women say they want to engage in politics until recently. What does this say? It is difficult to pinpoint one thing we need to do in society to make sure more women seek office as there are a myriad of reasons fewer women seek office or are elected. It is important to have young women see women seeking office—but they also need to see those women being treated fairly and with respect. Unfortunately, the political climate right now is when young women speak up, they are criticized so vehemently that it becomes a barrier to their participation. Who would want to go into a job where every time you speak up you are unfairly criticized? Women who seek office are criticized for their vocation, for what they wear, their size and culture and more. Women, who are raising children, see the barriers of a political job. The expectations are much different for women than for men in politics.

For any person considering entering politics, I think it is important to ask lots of questions before forming an opinion. Do not believe everything you read or hear or jump on a bandwagon quickly. Read, wait, listen to what others are saying, and then analyze through a critical lens before forming your own opinion. There are generally multiple perspectives to a situation or story. Critical analysis is of the utmost importance in politics along with critical reflection. This can be difficult in a society where people want answers and responses quickly, but it is paramount to take the time to analyze and reflect.

I had a number of portfolios while in government and I was on the treasury board for the full duration of my term. I feel good that I was able to have the provincial portion of the HST removed from feminine care products in our government's first budget. As the only woman on the board, my male colleagues were uncomfortable with me talking about this at first but totally supported having it removed.

While Minister of Education, I looked at best practices and research to inform what was the best way to support children in Nova Scotia being successful. We were seeing the trend of children falling behind and not finishing school. Research on student success informs us that if a student is behind by grade three, they will never catch up—even with support. Children who engaged in early education opportunities had a head start on children who did not have the same opportunity. Our government recognized that a universal early childhood program would provide all children the same opportunities. After much work within government, the Education Department and staff from early childhood centres we were able to launch five pilot programs in the province to discover best practices for Nova Scotia to move forward with a universal play-based curriculum so that every child in the province had the same opportunities. We implemented the SchoolsPlus program (a collaborative interagency approach) which was being piloted when we were elected. I am pleased to see it continue as it connects all of the various programs and services children and their families need.

We also expanded the program Options and Opportunities. Our government recognized the need for testing to identify strengths and weaknesses so that educators can develop strategies to support and help the student. The grade twelve standardized tests were discontinued as they were getting in the way of scholarships or placements in post-secondary placements. Testing moved to grade ten so that the results would inform the teachers, the student, and the parents of what each student needed in terms of support for them to be successful. This is an example of listening to teachers and parents and having the opportunity to make the change.

One of the fun things I got to achieve for my community while in office was the ability to have a sign placed on a new overpass on the 101 Highway—naming it the Freddie Wilson Overpass. One of the icons of the Annapolis Valley is resident Freddie Wilson, who stands on the overpass daily waving at cars as they enter the Valley. Giving him this recognition means a lot to people in the valley and it makes me happy every time I drive to and from the Annapolis Valley.

One of the things that I really liked about being in politics was the privilege as an MLA has to visit people in their homes. At every opportunity I would go to different areas in the constituency and meet with people at the door. It was a way for me to hear concerns and ideas. I never took for granted the privilege of being able to do that. Many people shared intimate stories of their lives with me. I met with people in celebration and in grief and everything in between. I am still in contact with many people I met as an MLA because you make such an authentic connection when you are meeting with them in their own home. It was such a privilege and an honour to be an elected member of the legislature and I appreciate having the opportunity to serve the people of Kings South and Nova Scotia as an MLA.

Photo courtesy of Brooks of Canada, from Pam Birdsall

31. PAM BIRDSALL
NDP MLA FOR LUNENBURG 2009–2013

I have always been political, but it was only after a lot of consideration that I decided to throw my hat into the ring. I was the chair of Second Story Women's Centre, which is one of the oldest [women and gendered-oppressed peoples' centres] in the province. At that time, we had a federal grant to do a project about women living in poverty in rural Nova Scotia. I heard from some of these women, what they were facing on a day-to-day basis. A lot of it was poverty and domestic abuse. It was older women who had been made invisible in society. As a New Democrat, our philosophy is, 'what I want for myself, I want for everyone.' That means I want people to have healthcare, and not to be abused and starving in Nova Scotia at a time like this. I was a member of the NDP, and a number of people said, "Pam, you should run! You should run!" As a business owner and a member of the creative economy, I did have a unique voice to offer.

Often the perennial response from a woman who is asked to run is, "I don't know. Let me think about it. Let me talk to whomever I need to talk to." Whereas if you ask a man, often they say, "Sure! No worries. I can do that." I was in a unique position because I co-own a company, so I really had to talk to my business partner. My husband was very involved in the party and the NDP executive so he said, "You should do it. You can do it. It's certainly within your skillset." All said and done, the impetus was really women's issues and women being politically marginalized and knowing that there are not a lot of women in government speaking our story. In Lunenburg County, which was my constituency, I was the third woman elected. The first woman was a Conservative, Maxine Cochran. The second woman was a Liberal, Lila O'Connor. I felt honoured to be in their company. They were both women I respected.

Politics is still pretty sexist. You have to really prove yourself. You have to speak louder, and you have to be more articulate. You have to try to be smarter than most people around you. I always felt I had to prove myself more than the men in the room. Just by being in the room, you would not even say anything, and they say, "We know what you're going to say Pam." Of course, they do not, but assumptions are made.

I will never forget the first Remembrance Day I was in office. It was a Remembrance Day parade and the first one [I went to] was here in Mahone Bay. I had never walked in a Remembrance Day parade, and I thought well, the legion wears navy blazers and grey pants, so I wore a navy-blue blazer, grey pants, a poppy, red leather gloves and red lipstick. The comments were, "Well her lipstick was awfully red." Seriously, if you are asking what sort of things women come up against that men do not? I cannot imagine them saying, "Did you see the color of his socks?" Sexism goes from broad strokes: 'She's a woman, let her prove herself,' to fine points like, 'Her lipstick is a bit too red.' You think, *Truly? Is this the way people judge you?* I have even gotten, "I voted for you because I like your hair." Thank you, I guess!

The whole thing was an honour. It truly was a deep honour to represent people in the Lunenburg constituency. Having been the owner of a gallery shop, people self-edited when they came into our shop. I did not see a broad swath of the community. One of the things that was most profound for me was my personal understanding and appreciation for people who live in Lunenburg. I spent a lot of time doing my homework going to all these different parts of the constituency to meet the people there.

I tried to represent people in a way that was different than what they had seen before. I was in the paper every week, because I went everywhere. If someone invited me somewhere, I would go. If someone wanted to see me, they could come and see. I would find it quite eye-opening when people would say, "All we had to do is call last week and here we are?" I would say, "Yeah? I'm your MLA. I am supposed to represent you whether you voted for me or not." It seemed that response was not what had always happened, certainly not to the degree that I wanted it to happen.

I think I confounded a lot of people. For example, the Christmas tree growers—because Lunenburg is known as the Christmas Tree Capital of the World—it is a very big deal here. Several times a year they would have these technical sessions. MLAs would be invited from the area. Some would come, shake hands, and leave. I would sit there and take notes. After awhile, I knew them all. Once, in the New Germany area there was a huge problem with a particular dirt road. The trucks [carrying the trees] weighed tonnes, driving uphill on these gravel roads that really were not well gravelled, and they would be sliding off the road. Eventually the truck drivers were refusing to move the product. At one point, I had three Christmas tree growing companies come to talk to me and say, "What can we do about this road?" I got the Department of Transportation people together with our Minister of Economic Development and said, "Okay this is my problem. How can we solve this?" The deputy ministers often hated to see me come. I am a creative person and I think outside of the box. In this job I was not working in clay, I was working with people's problems. We did, much to a lot of eyebrow-raising and the chagrin of a lot of people who would have said, "We've never done this before," go in and solve that problem creatively. I asked them to treat it like a triage, and they fixed the road. That story is exemplary of what I was able to do. Get in on the ground and find solutions that make sense. A lot of the Christmas tree growers I still see around say, "That road is still holding up!"

As the only professional artist/craftsperson in our NDP caucus, I was profoundly interested in the creative economy initiatives. Ten years before we became government, the former government dissolved the arts council which oversaw and helped in the disbursement of funding and grants from the province. I was asked to chair the committee which created the terms of reference to create the new body now known as Arts Nova Scotia. This was applauded by the members of the arts community. I was also a member of the legislation committee which created the Status of the Artists Act which was passed into legislation in 2011. Both of these endeavours gave me great personal satisfaction.

Women need to be at the table. They need to be heard. I am sure that's what every woman you have talked to who has put themselves forward in government has said to you.

When there is equal power things will shift. Dramatically.

People really have to question what their motives are. What is my motive? Why am I doing this? If it is for self-aggrandizement, politics is not the way to go. You are not in it for yourself, and you should not be. If that is your motivation, do something else. It has got to be for the higher good. Being a member of the first NDP government in our province will always be a highlight of my life. I learned so much, and it was an honour to call Premier Darrell Dexter a friend.

Photo courtesy of Nova Scotia Legislature

32. LENORE ZANN
NDP MLA FOR TRURO-BIBLE HILL-MILLBROOK-SALMON RIVER 2009–2019
LIBERAL MP FOR CUMBERLAND COLCHESTER 2019–PRESENT

John Lennon once famously said, "Life is what happens to you while you're busy making other plans." I can certainly relate. I was born in Sydney, Australia in 1959. I was an only child and in 1968, my parents Janice and Paul Zann, both teachers, decided to emigrate to Canada along with 2,000 other teachers, following a call by Prime Minister Pierre Trudeau. That year, there was a need for teachers in Canada and the Baby Boom was still in full swing.

I knew at an early age that I wanted to be a professional actor—although growing up in rural Nova Scotia, the bright lights of Broadway and Hollywood, or even Toronto or Vancouver, seemed like a distant dream. Especially when I had no vocal training or acting lessons. Instead, I simply sang at the top of my lungs to the cows while roaming the fields of Belmont, writing all manner of poems and short stories.

However, after winning a public speaking contest in grade eight at Onslow Junior High, I was then cast in three consecutive lead roles in the annual high school musicals at Cobequid Educational Centre in Truro by my guidance counsellor, Norman Hines, followed by further leads in amateur musical productions at the KIPAWO Showboat Theatre Company. I was ready for 'prime time,' playing small roles at Neptune Theatre in Halifax for $75 a week. After two summers working at Neptune between high school years, I was qualified to receive my first Canadian Actors' Equity Card. I was a fully-fledged 'professional actor' and a proud Union member by the time I turned seventeen.

That September of 1977, I left home for Toronto (by train—right from the Truro Railway Station) to attend York University's drama program and study political science, consolidating my two biggest passions: arts and politics. While in Toronto I auditioned for Canada's first and only theatre that was focused on producing original Canadian musicals each year, Prince Edward Island's Charlottetown Festival, famed for the musical *Anne of Green Gables*.

That was truly a golden summer—performing in musicals, hanging out with my fellow cast mates till late in the night and spending days off together at the beautiful beaches, with many deep conversations about our dreams, singing songs, weaving tales, and sharing bonfires well into the night under the stars. Every year at the end of summer, the Charlottetown Festival produces a big fundraising concert. It was at this concert event that I was "discovered" by composer/playwright Cliff Jones from Toronto. It turned out he had written a rock-opera based on the life and untimely death of the legendary Marilyn Monroe, called "Hey Marilyn!" He had been searching for an entire year for the right actress to play the starring role.

I walked out on stage that night having played small roles all summer but I had decided to perform "The Cornet Man," made famous by Barbara Streisand. I belted that song out at the top of my lungs to 1,100 people as if I was singing in the cow fields in Belmont. When the song ended and the crowd jumped to their feet for a standing ovation to end act one of the concert, Cliff Jones and his wife Eve recall they simply turned to each other and said, "That's Marilyn!" I was nineteen.

That production, which opened in January of 1980, kickstarted my professional acting career. For the next twenty-nine years I performed across Canada, the United States, Australia, and Europe. My childhood dream actually came true. Of course none of it was easy and as is with most artists, there were many highs and lows. But that makes you appreciate everything even more.

My first big break in animation came in 1992, back in Toronto where I was cast as Rogue in the popular 90s animated *X-Men* series. That show became a global sensation and thirty years later is one of the two top animated series in history. Rogue is the strongest woman in the universe. She is sassy and sexy, but compassionate and cares for the underdog. She is also a loner and totally devoted to her work trying to improve society, stop discrimination, and stand up for those who are bullied or maligned because she has been bullied and abused herself and is often underestimated because she's a woman. I related to her immensely.

During my thirty years as a performer while I travelled extensively around the world and across North America. With my longtime interest in politics as well as the arts, I took the time to learn about different governance structures as well as the varied cultural, political, and spiritual customs. After all that traveling, it became clear to me that humans all have more in common than we have differences. We may look somewhat different but we all want the same things: to be happy, healthy, peaceful and safe. And we want that for our children. We need to work together to make life better for everybody on this tiny little blue planet—to protect Mother Nature and our most valuable natural resources: clean water and air. We must not squander these resources.

After my time in New York I decided it was time to move home to Nova Scotia and give back to my community. I wanted to teach a whole new generation of young artists that they could be successful no matter what small town or village they came from, if they believed in themselves, were willing to work diligently, and never let anybody tell them it couldn't be done. In 2007, I bought a house in Truro near both my parents and sister's family. There's no place like home.

In 2008, there was a financial crisis and I remember looking at the front page of the *Globe and Mail*. There was a circle of world leaders in the photograph and all of them were males—except for Angela Merkel of Germany. I thought, *What is wrong with this picture? Why aren't there more women at the table to be part of the decision-making at a time of crisis?*

That's when I first thought perhaps I should run for elected office. Alexa McDonough was a very dear friend of mine at the time. She had taken me under her wing when I was younger. It was International Women's Day and Alexa had invited me to job-shadow her. She brought me to the legislature in Halifax for the very first time; I was probably twenty-four. At that time she was the only woman and the only NDP member in the Nova Scotia House of Assembly.

I sat in the west gallery and noticed immediately that Alexa was on her feet giving an impassioned speech while all of the men around her were paying no attention. They were instead ensconced in the serious business of throwing paper airplanes at each other. That was my first experience with politics in person. I was floored. And I was angry. That experience planted the seed in my mind that maybe someday I would be down in the trenches with other feminists fighting for what was right. For equality. For social justice. For Mother Earth. For the public good. Years later when the NDP asked me to run in my hometown of Truro, I thought about it for about a year. Everyone told me I would be crazy to run for the NDP in Truro—even my own mother! The region had been a Conservative stronghold for over a hundred years.

When I first decided to run for political office in 2009, some people said, "Oh what would an actor know about politics?" It turns out I knew a lot about politics—and people. As ten years as a provincial member of the legislative assembly of Nova Scotia have proved: four years in the first majority NDP government in Nova Scotia, and six years as an opposition critic with eleven different critic portfolios. And now one year more as a member of parliament as well.

Within three hours of the announcement that I was running for the nomination, we discovered that one of the opposition parties had sent a picture of me from a scene in the American TV series, *The L-Word* to the CBC six o'clock news. They had taken a freeze-frame from a scene in which my role called for nudity. I had already told the NDP in my disclosure statement that as a professional actor for thirty years, I had done nude scenes. It was part of my job. The very next day the media descended upon Truro and chased every little old lady they could find to try and get a quote on how terrible this was—and to their surprise every single person they asked said, "What are you talking about? She is an actor! That's her job! This is the twenty-first century!" I was so proud of my hometown.

The opposition researchers must have thought they had hit the mother lode when they started researching me, but it completely backfired. I won the 2009 election in a landslide. One headline announced, "It's a Zannslide!" I was proud to be part of the first-ever NDP government in Nova Scotia.

When I was running that time, Alexa McDonough, Rocky Jones, and my father Paul were the only people who had said, "I think you have a chance!"[12] They believed in me.

The NDP government fell in the following election in 2013. Out of the thirty-one NDP MLAs, only seven remained standing, I was the only backbencher that got re-elected. Even the premier had lost his seat. To be honest, since the six others had a pretty tight bond as former cabinet ministers, I felt a bit lonely. Once it was announced that there would be a leadership race, a number of New Democrat Party members asked me to run. In particular, those who cared about the environment supported me since I had been very vocal about my concerns about climate change, sustainable energy, and greenhouse gas emissions.

Once again, I asked former NDP Leader Alexa McDonough if she thought I should put my hat in the ring. She agreed to endorse me and so did another former leader, Helen MacDonald. I was the only woman to run for leader. That leadership race was interesting. I got to see how even within political parties people can turn on each other. And the closer you get to the seat of power, the nastier things can get.

Some within our small caucus seemed peeved that I was even running. Caucus staff were allowed to take sides and work on another candidate's campaign even while we were still all working together as a caucus. That's very hard. How can you maintain caucus solidarity under those conditions? Whisper campaigns were started against me. Walking into the caucus office, I often felt like some wished I would just disappear into a hole in the ground. The workplace became toxic. It was a very difficult and painful time. One of my MLA colleagues, Denise Peterson Rafuse, noticed what was happening and decided it was unfair and started supporting me.[13] We worked hard, but in the end, I came second. I immediately threw my support in for the new leader, Gary Burrill.

In total I won three elections provincially for the NDP in Truro-Bible Hill-Millbrook-Salmon River from 2009–2019 even though I had been warned each time that it would be impossible to be elected in Truro. I think the results prove that people in Northern Nova Scotia often vote for the person—not the party. We vote for those who are not afraid to speak their mind and who are prepared to stand up for shared principles and values, even if it means we stand alone. That is what I have done both provincially and now federally since becoming member of parliament for Cumberland-Colchester.

I was asked to run federally by MP Bill Casey, as he had decided to retire.[14] After a long soul search and many discussions with my parents, friends, and constituents, I resigned from the NDP and announced I was planning to run federally for the Liberal Party of Canada under the leadership of Prime Minister Justin Trudeau. I was successful in the election in 2019 and became only the second woman ever to represent this federal riding in Ottawa. I am still standing up and speaking out (both inside caucus and publicly) about the causes I believe in.

However, in the first six months of my tenure as MP, my federal constituency of Cumberland-Colchester experienced the most challenging and horrific events ever imaginable—events that brought

---

[12] Rocky Jones was an African-Nova Scotian lawyer from Truro who was internationally known for his advocacy for human rights, poverty, and race.

[13] Denise Peterson-Rafuse was the MLA for Chester-St. Margaret's from 2009-2017.

[14] MP Bill Casey had served as a Conservative, an Independent, and retired as a Liberal.

us to our knees. On top of the global Covid-19 pandemic and the resulting lockdown in Nova Scotia, the largest mass shooting in Canada's history took place in many of our small, picturesque, rural communities. The harm done is deep. It will take us a very long time to recover from the shock and trauma of the tragic events of April 18th and 19th, 2020.

However, in spite of everything I have jumped into action in Ottawa, introducing a federal version of my initial provincial Private Members Bill 111, An Act to Address Environmental Racism, which was hailed as the first of its kind. It reached Second Reading in Province House, but did not pass.

This year, 2020, I introduced to the House of Commons in Ottawa Bill C-230, A National Strategy to Redress Environmental Racism Act. It was Seconded by Green Party Leader Elizabeth May and has been endorsed by Dr. David Suzuki, and is expected to return to the House for Second Reading. That is very exciting and it is my hope that this time as a member of government, with the support of other parties, Bill C-230 will pass into law.

My advice to all women considering running for office in all levels of government is: DO IT. We need your compassion, clear vision, and passion. It's the only way things will ever change. It is my sincere hope that my shoulders are broad enough for other women to climb upon so that our ladder becomes a bridge for more and more women. Together we can create a positive, loving, safe, mutually-respectful, violence-free and environmentally healthy future for our children, our elders, and the generations to come.

Photo by Mosy Photography

33. JOYCE TREEN
LIBERAL MLA FOR COLE HARBOUR-EASTERN PASSAGE 2013–2017

I have been living in the community of Eastern Passage for over forty years and have always been very active in my community even as a young teenager. Over the years, I have been involved in our summer carnival, Girl Guides, volunteering with my church, and on many committees and boards. I had also owned a small business in the community for almost thirty years. I have always been committed to making Eastern Passage a better place for everyone. It really is a special place to live.

Back in 2013 one of the major projects in my life was working on was bringing a high school to our community. I had been working on the project for fifteen years along with many others that felt we needed and deserved our own high school. Our children had been sent to fill schools in other communities for many years. Issues like early bus times, limitations to extra help, and extracurricular activities lead us to advocate for change.

This was about the time when several people approached me to ask if I would be interested in running for the MLA for Cole Harbour-Eastern Passage. I had not given much thought to running for elected office to be honest. Stephen McNeil, leader of the Nova Scotia Liberal Party, came to me and wanted to talk about that possibility. We had a conversation where I had the chance to tell him about my passion for the community and the importance of a high school to our children and families. I remember telling him how crucial the new school was to our community and that he should be prepared that I was going to fight for it. As it turns out, he accepted my terms and we signed the nomination papers.

Being fairly new to the process of an election and all the details, it definitely had a steep learning curve. My entrepreneurial spirit is what helped me through all the steps. After becoming elected it was a humbling experience to sit at my desk in the legislature representing the communities of Cole Harbour, Eastern Passage, and South Woodside.

Politics needs the diversity of many views to make good legislation. In 2013 there were a lot of great, strong women elected into government. I developed wonderful friendships with some of these women, who also became mentors. Margaret Miller, Suzanne Lohnes-Croft, and I could always be found together. People called us the three musketeers.

If you asked me if being a woman stood in the way of my journey, I would say no, but politics is still a bit of an old boys' club. For example, I distinctly remember a moment when I was with two of my male colleagues. We were out somewhere and two men came over and made introductions to my colleagues, but not to me. It was like I was not even standing there. It was really short sighted because some of the hardest working MLAs were the women members in my caucus. Though, the women of our caucus always knew their value because our Premier Stephen McNeil reminded us often.

Getting the high school built in our community of Eastern Passage is what I am most proud of. It was a long journey with many people helping over the years. Many of those people's children aged out and they were no longer as committed. Me? I'm more of a dog with a bone. If I say I am going to do something and I have set my mind to it, I am committed to the end.

My second greatest accomplishment during my time as MLA was the service dog legislation. A constituent, Medric Cousineau, who had a service dog named Thai, came and met with me. He brought to my attention the inability for people with disabilities using a working dog to access public places. At that point, there were no rules about handlers and their service dogs, only for teams of the visually impaired. Having the chance to chat with that community member about the importance of service dogs and making public spaces accessible to all started me down the road to advocate for change. I brought the issue to government and there was initially some push back. It had not been on their radar but I kept pushing. Being an entrepreneur, you learn that you have to work hard or you will not move forward. Continuing to advocate and educate government members, a few years later I was very happy to have been a key person for a piece of legislation that is making a big difference in the quality of peoples' lives.

It is easy to be intimidated by the world of politics. All of the procedures and lingo, the way people talk…it can certainly be daunting. As a newcomer you can quickly feel out of your depths and shy away from asking questions. What I would tell anyone just starting out is to dig right in and ask your questions. Everyone is important and everyone has a role to play. Each and every one of us has the power to make a difference. I remember one day sitting on the Law Amendments Committee hearing from Nova Scotians on the proposed ban on flavoured tobacco products. There was a young girl, about eleven or twelve years old, who came to speak to the committee. At that point some of us were on the fence about some of the proposed changes. When that young girl spoke, she talked from the heart about protecting her generation against the harmful effects of tobacco. That all flavour should be banned. She was inspirational; she changed the legislation. That one girl. She was amazing.

It was only when [Grace and Sarah] came to me about this book that I learned I was one of the first fifty women elected in Nova Scotia, I had no idea. It was a 'wow' moment and it brought a smile to my face. My advice to other women would be if you want to do this, you should follow your dream and do it. I never thought growing up that I would ever be in politics. I came from a poor family, we lived on welfare when I was younger. My father died when I was six so there were all kinds of struggles on the way that changed my direction several times in my life. Politics can be a nasty beast, but at the end of the day I truly feel it is one of the main venues to make change. If you thought about taking this journey, my advice to you is to take a deep breath and do it. You might not know it right away, I know I did not, but looking back, being able to help people with their challenges was addictive. With every person I helped it inspired me to work that much harder.

I loved my time as the MLA for Cole Harbour-Eastern Passage and all the wonderful people I met during my time. When I close my eyes and look back, I am proud of my accomplishments and the work our government did.

I was honoured to represent the people of Cole Harbour, Cow Bay, Eastern Passage, Shearwater, and South Woodside.

Photo by Mosy Photography

34. The HONOURABLE JOANNE BERNARD
LIBERAL MLA FOR DARTMOUTH NORTH 2013–2017
Minister of Community Services and Housing Nova Scotia, responsible for the Disabled Persons Commissions Act and for the Advisory Council on the Status of Women

My background is mostly in the non-profit sector, but I have wanted to run for public office since the age of eight. I had written a letter to Pierre Elliott Trudeau protesting the seal hunt and someone wrote me back. That just sparked something in me at that age where I thought, *you know what? I can make a difference somewhere. I can have my voice be used*. So, as I grew older, my academic journey took me into political science, and I have a master's degree in political science from Acadia. Then life happened. Life happened with a little boy and a divorce and a period of struggling. My career in non-profit was mostly working with women either leaving domestic violence or trying to overcome addictions. It was not until I was in my late forties when the personal, the political, and the private all came together. I turned fifty on the campaign trail in 2013.

I used to work for the NDP caucus back in the late 90s. I had followed Stephen [McNeil]. I started watching Stephen and Diana [Whalen] and I really liked their style. To me, they were both folksy, they could relate well, and everything that they were talking about resonated with me. I first approached Diana and said, "You know, I'm really thinking of going for the nomination in Dartmouth North. I don't know any of the riding association, I'm not a Liberal Party member, but I work in the community and I live in the community. I felt I could step up and have a solid chance of winning. It was a culmination of a lot of factors at the same time that said, "You know what, you can do this."

I did not put my name forward until I sat down with my son and my partner because I was well aware that where I am a lesbian, it would be an issue. And it was. I wanted to make sure that she was okay with that, and I wanted to make sure that he was okay with that. And so, once I got their blessing it was full steam ahead. I was the second nominated candidate in the province for the Liberals in 2013 so I had about an eighteen-month head start.

Once I got elected and I realized that being a politician who was "out" was a new thing. The fact that I was appointed to cabinet made me historical in that sense that no other cabinet minister had ever been openly gay. I remember one of the proudest days of my life was introducing my wife from the gallery of the legislature. Every person in that legislature stood up, across party lines. It was important. People understood the importance of that moment, and I wanted it read-in to Hansard.

I dealt with homophobia, I have dealt with misogyny, and I have dealt with being the minister of a very difficult portfolio [Community Services]. You become the face of a very intimate relationship with people who need your services. Nobody called that department on a good day. It was constant, constant strife. I got death threats. I was harassed and bullied. I had a security detail at one point in my ministerialship. I was fat-shamed. It was very, very difficult on my family, and on me. It was not until the end of 2017 that I revealed publicly that I had lived with an eating disorder for twenty years. I talked about my eating disorder and being fat-shamed and how those are triggers. I started fighting back, especially to online bullying. I would screenshot everything and put it back out there—especially if names were attached to it. And I have done lots of talks, both since being elected and being defeated, talking about my experiences and what young women can do in terms of protecting themselves and more importantly, not normalizing the violence against women in politics. Whenever I hear, 'you've gotta have a thick skin,' I cringe, because you're normalizing that violence and that is absolutely not okay.

I went on TV in 2015 because I was getting harassed. It was around that time when marriage equality in the United States came through. I could see the homophobia ramping up in all three of my offices. I just drew a line in the sand and did an interview on *Live at 5*. I talked about how if this is a cabinet minister being bullied and harassed for her sexuality, what is happening in rural Nova Scotia to the young thirteen- and fourteen-year-old kids who know that they are gay and are not living the lives they need to live? It became very personal for me. For young women coming into this, I say eyes wide open. Know that you are going to be a target. Know that you are going to be judged for how you look, what you wear, what you say. I did not want to reveal my eating disorder because I thought that in politics, which is a blood sport, that it would characterize me as having a weakness. I already had so much on my plate, and well, I did not want anyone to say—and it is terrible to think—'Jesus, she can't even do an eating disorder right. She's still fat.' Because I got so much judgement as my performance as a minister or an MLA that I just did not need that very personal journey to be judged.

I guess one of the big regrets that I have is that my parents always knew that I wanted to run for office, and they were not here for that. I wish that they had seen that destiny that I had chosen as an eight-year-old, because they heard about it forever. I am proud of the work that we did as a government. I am still proud of the work the government does. I am proud of the work I did as a minister. I took a life experience of being on income assistance for nine years and taking that experience to try to make a system that's better. I can see the fruition of that now. So that was really important to me. You know, I have been asked a lot to speak to young women and I enjoy doing that. I miss government, I do not miss politics. They are two very different things.

I am very proud of legislation that has gone through [in my time], and the sexual violence strategy. I posted a picture yesterday, it was six years since Kelly [Regan], Diana [Whalen], Lena [Metlege Diab], Karen [Casey] and I made history. We were the most women ever to be appointed to cabinet, the first female deputy premier, the first female attorney general, and the first openly gay cabinet minister—those were important milestones back then. I think that I have been part of helping to pave that way. And I have a granddaughter now. So if my granddaughter ever, ever, ever, chooses to do public service through elected office, I hope somewhere along the line I have made it easier for her.

From L to R: Hon. Lena Metlege Diab, Hon. Joanne Bernard, Hon. Karen Casey, Hon. Kelly Regan, Hon. Diana Whalen at cabinet swearing-in ceremony in 2013.

35. The HONOURABLE PATRICIA ARAB
LIBERAL MLA FOR FAIRVIEW-CLAYTON PARK 2013–PRESENT
Minister of Service Nova Scotia and Internal Services and Communications Nova Scotia

I was a teacher and a guidance counsellor prior to entering politics. I got involved in party politics when I was twelve and my father's friend, Gerry Fogarty, was running for MLA in our area. He took me down to the campaign headquarters where I was promptly put to work stuffing envelopes and helping out. When I got to university, Mr. Fogarty was the Speaker of the House, and he asked me if I would be interested in the Page Program. I put my name forward and I became a page and messenger in the galleries. It was there where I met some amazing friends who got me involved with the Young Liberals at Dalhousie University. It's important to note that I always looked at politics as a hobby, I never wanted to have a career in politics. I was never someone who was interested in being a staffer or going to Ottawa. My involvement was always just for fun.

My mom and dad were both strong community activists. [They] spent a lot of time helping new immigrants that would come to town, members of our church community, our neighbours, and really anyone who did not know how to navigate the system—individuals who would never think to call their MLA or city councillor. When my mother got sick in 2011, she wasn't able to continue serving others in the same way. Knowing that she was not getting any better, I turned my focus, not on what I would do without my mother, but instead, who is going to be there to help others when she is gone? She was in the hospital, her phone rang and there was somebody who needed help on an issue they were having. Instead of ignoring the call, she passed the phone to me and asked, "Can you take care of this?" This was the essence of who my mom was.

I decided then that I wanted to find a way to be that person who people in the community would call. I originally thought that maybe the best move would be to run for city council. However, in April of 2012 my mom passed, and then my dad suddenly passed two months after her. By the time the municipal election came around, that fall, I really was not thinking about running for anything. It was shortly after that election while attending a fundraising dinner for the Liberal Party when someone asked me when I was going to run. I told them how I had been thinking about running, and even though circumstances in my family had made me rethink, I still wanted to do something in public service in honour of them. Kelly Regan heard me tell my story, pulled me aside and said, "Have you ever considered running for us provincially?"

I did not think about it too much—I did not think about what the consequences may be. I just thought, "You know what? This is a good way to help people. It's a good way to make meaning of my parents' death." I joke a lot that a normal person after losing both parents would just go talk to a counsellor. I decided to run for public office. If I had allowed myself five minutes to think about it, I would have talked myself out of it. I would have talked about all the reasons why someone my age should not be running for public office—wanting to have a family, or having a young family. There would be a million reasons not to do it if you think about it too much. Then you miss out. There are a lot of examples now, particularly in the federal government where young women can run, have a full family life, and be able to time manage. You can have all of those things. You do not have to sacrifice one for the other.

If you are thinking too much about it, you are going to wear yourself out and think, 'there's no way I can be good at both. I'll just end up being mediocre at one or the other.' And decide not to do it. But that really is not the case. You can do both and you can be great at both. We need to give ourselves more credit.

I am one of the youngest female MLAs in this province's history. They came and told me after the [cabinet] swearing-in ceremony that I was the youngest female cabinet minister. **It is definitely a benchmark that needs to be broken.**

Always remember that it is not just about running for public office. We need more women involved in agencies, boards, and commissions. We need women to be sitting at policy-making tables. We need more women to be part of the civil service. Running is one aspect of it, but there are many steps along that way that will allow you to make impactful change. We do not have enough voices sitting at any of those tables. Make your voice heard and put yourself at the table!

Photo by Mosy Photography

36. The HONOURABLE LENA METLEGE DIAB
LIBERAL MLA FOR HALIFAX ARMDALE 2013–PRESENT
Minister of Justice and First Female Attorney General
Minister of Immigration
Ministre des Affaires acadiennes et de la Francophonie
Minister of Labour and Advanced Education

I come from a cultural community—I am of Lebanese origin. Before entering politics, I practiced law in a law firm in Halifax. Professions like law can be very male dominated. The thing I really had going for me was that I had lots of family support—my mom and my dad were my number one fans.

I am the oldest of six children. We are five girls and a boy, so we were very much a girl-dominated household. My father and mother—the number one thing that they taught us was education, education, education. As long as you are educated, then no matter what happens to you later, you can work and make a living and support yourself. That was empowerment—knowledge and education.

I was the first woman justice minister in the province of Nova Scotia. I did not believe that, and in fact the premier did not know, and when he called and said he wanted to name me [minister] he said, "I didn't know this, we're not sure, we're looking at it." They looked at it, and I was named the first female attorney general and Minister of Justice for Nova Scotia, after what? Two hundred and some years?

I have seen real wars, I escaped wars twice in my life. Just doing what I am doing now, knowing all of the obstacles and challenges that have come my way all these years, it gives me that much drive to want to help people. Really, that is the most important thing that I could do. Being somebody who comes from an immigrant family and could not speak a word of English until I was eleven…not only becoming an MLA, but now being named to the immigration portfolio and the Office of Acadian Affairs and Francophonie, gives me such a perspective on issues around us provincially, nationally, and globally.

I cannot wait every morning to get out of bed, so that I can start the day helping people. Whether it is one on one helping people as an MLA or helping groups of people on certain issues in certain portfolios. I just love it. It keeps me going.

But still, my most important achievement is the fact that I am a mother and now I have grandchildren. Regardless of their sex, or what they want to be or what they are studying or where they are in life—the most important thing for me is to support them like I was supported when I was young from my parents and siblings. I think that is one thing we can do as a community is to support each other. If communities can do that…this province has so many opportunities in the youth that we have. I see it every day. We have to ensure that people see that and help each other.

It is interesting, but reflecting on my life, I have always been involved in the political process, since high school, for over thirty-five years now. Although I had twenty years of legal practice, I took an avid interest in politics. The fact that I had an established life and knew the relationships between government, business, etc., was a great asset to me. I felt I had something to contribute. I appreciate so much that my parents were enthusiastic and encouraged me. My family was very supportive throughout.

Serving people was my calling. When I made the decision to enter politics and won the riding of Halifax Armdale in October 2013 and was appointed to the cabinet, I knew I wanted to make a difference in my riding and provide more opportunities for our young people. I have to say that when the premier contacted me and told me that I was being given the justice and immigration files, I did not know what to think. I told myself that these were two files that were an integral part of my life and that were very much like me. I think the biggest and most beautiful surprise was to see the confidence that people had in me by entrusting me with two major files from this government.

I admit that I love what I do today as much as I did when I first started. I have learnt a great deal. My greatest thrill is the interaction with people in my riding, in Nova Scotia, across the country and internationally. I was in Paris last week for important meetings that help shape the future of our country and our province. You know, when I was a little girl, I went to school in Lebanon and the second language I learned was French. When I returned to Nova Scotia at the age of eleven, I started learning English. Languages have become an important part of my work.

The most gratifying part of my work is making a difference, I feel privileged to be able to represent a culture, a people and an identity. It is important, because without culture or identity, we don't exist. It is culture and identity that anchors us and shapes us. The links between my own culture and Acadian culture for instance makes me feel at home here. We share common values.

Although I love my work, I have learned that in politics, no matter what you do, you can never do enough. The good thing about it is that it pushes you to always look for something better. The disadvantage is that people tend to look for the negative. To quote Winston Churchill, "Never look for challenges in opportunities but rather look for opportunities in challenges." For my part, I was brought up with the idea that every challenge offers an opportunity to learn and grow.

For anyone looking to become a potential candidate in politics, I say you must really want to serve people to the best of your ability. You must know that there will be challenges and sacrifices. You will work hard. Politics has taken up a lot of space in my life, but I have been fortunate to have the blessing and support of my parents and children and great people around me. I am a mother, and before I got into politics, I never missed an appointment for my children, whether it was for school or the doctor. So if you have a family, I think it is important to include them in the decision-making process.

As a woman in politics, I have experienced some challenges. I am a mother, and I have had to juggle my work and family life. I am a lawyer, and in my professional life I have always had to build my self-confidence and my strength in a man's world. Through my education and my career, I believe that I have a certain authority, but as a leader in a man's world, I have had to create a shell for myself. Because of my education, I have always focused my attention on my development, and above all I have worked hard.

Photo by Mosy Photography

37. The HONOURABLE MARGARET MILLER
LIBERAL MLA FOR HANTS EAST 2013–PRESENT
Minister of Environment
Minister of Natural Resources

My husband Robert and I owned and operated a dairy farm for twenty-five years, starting when I was nineteen! During that time, I also had a home-based business—a ceramics shop in my house. That took over much of my time until I became allergic to dust. Shortly after we sold the farm to another Dutch immigrant. When we moved, we built [a home] just across from the farm on 200 acres, and I quickly got bored. I started another small business after trying to get rid of my fabric stash. I loved to sew so took some quilting classes and loved the creativity of quilting. Before long, my hobby turned to a quilting business and I was teaching classes three times a week.

In 2004, on the night of my fiftieth birthday, we got a phone call. Our son was in a crash in PEI. The next day, he was declared dead. I found out at the hospital that the driver had been drunk, and later on found out that his blood alcohol had been three times the legal limit, and he was doing 178 kilometres an hour when he hit Bruce and Jason in their vehicle. My son, Bruce, was killed by a drunk driver. That changed my life.

You cannot do anything about what happened, but you can do something about what is going to happen. So, I had started asking the questions, "Why are there so many drunk drivers?" If the drunk driver had lived…chances are at that time he would have gotten house arrest. I said, "He can murder my son and he can get house arrest?" It just did not make sense. So, the question was, "Who does something about this? This is ridiculous, this cannot happen. It has affected my life, my children, my future."

I got involved in Mothers Against Drunk Driving two weeks after Bruce's death. I started speaking to classes and sharing my story and telling them about Bruce, what he did as a police officer, about impaired driving in his own community, how he had been hit and how he was killed. I did that for a few years and then I was asked to think about applying to be the national president of MADD Canada. What better way could I pay tribute to my son than to tell his story at a national level? So, I applied, and I was successful.

I made sure my presentations as president were going to be effective. I served in that role for three years, and spoke to literally thousands and thousands of children at schools. My goal was to make them cry, to make them feel and to make them remember what I was there to say, and I did. Bruce's story was told in a video that went to over a million children. It was called *Friday Night*. I was finishing my two-year term, and they asked me to stay a third year. Then legally they have to change national presidents. During that time, I was feeling like I was ready to stop travelling, I was ready to stop speaking, but I felt I had more to tell, so I wrote a book. It's called: *The Gift: A MADD Mother's Journey of Healing*. It was not just my story. It starts with my story and then tells the story of eleven or twelve [others] from across Canada. We shared the stories and they were all different. I was doing interviews for the book after it was published, and Stephen McNeil heard me doing an interview.

Meanwhile, I had started doing some motivational speaking with young people in groups and a friend of mine had come up with me on a drive up to Gaspé, to a First Nations community. She said, "What political party do you support? You should think about politics." I said, "No, no, no." Part of my job as national president was as an activist and a lobbyist. She was trying to convince me that I should get involved in politics and, frankly, I thought she was crazy. She said, "Well what team would you play for?" I wasn't partisan. I voted for the person I best thought would represent my values at the time in my area. I had voted NDP, but was not happy with what was happening with their government. I had voted Conservative, but I did not like the Conservative leader in Nova Scotia at that point. So, I said, "I guess it would have to be Liberal." She told me I needed to meet her friend—who was Stephen McNeil. That drive was ten hours back and forth. She talked to me for five [hours] until I said I would talk to him.

She called Stephen and said, "I've got someone that you should talk to." And he told her that I was already on his list. We met one day for lunch, and I was very watchful of how he was with all the other people in the restaurant when he came in. The discussion that we had—which was not high pressure—was really cool. [He] was talking about the women in his life and how much they meant to him and how politics had changed, that [he feels] having more women in politics brings something different to the table. When I came out from that meeting, I thought, "Wow, maybe this is a good thing." He said, "I don't want just lawyers, I don't want just people that are into politics to become politicians. I want everyday Nova Scotians. I want people with different experiences and different life experiences." I thought about it for a month. After a month…well, I have never been more nervous, I was not even as nervous getting married as I was telling Stephen McNeil I would run.

I got involved because I wanted to be able to change things from inside Nova Scotia. One of those things was the Organ Transplant Act. That session was pretty emotional. We had donated Bruce's organs, even though he was not identified as an organ donor, so that change meant a lot to me.[15] Also, the impaired driving changes meant a lot. I was concerned that the graduated licensing program was only six months. Now it is a lot longer. Part of that is because when teenagers are first driving, they do not learn to drive in all four seasons. It gives you a chance to get more experience going in. And the zero-blood alcohol before five years of driving for everybody starts that trend that you do not drink and drive—period. You cannot have any alcohol or drugs in your system. Usually if people can get past that five years, they do not ever want to start. Drinking and driving was quite prevalent in rural Nova Scotia. It still is in a lot of areas in Nova Scotia, but now the fines and penalties are much more severe, and you do not see the death and injury as much as it once was. I think all of those things do help. I am still looking forward to doing more.

I also must say one of the [changes] with the biggest impact is going to be the Coastal Protection Act. That was not just me, but it was something I advocated for in my first round as environment [minister]. Iain [Rankin] took it over and did a lot of the bulk of the work when he was minister. By the time I came back to the ministry, it was pretty much ready to hit the gate. But I was really proud of that.

I hear women in many cases talk about the handicaps of being in politics or business. I have never felt that. I was always involved in the 4-H program, where you learn to do by doing, and I was very successful in that program. When I got married, we were equal partners in the farm. There was no sense of 'he's the boss and I'm not'—it was an equal discussion all the way through. When it came to any of our other businesses, it was the same thing. Coming into politics, I did not feel it was a handicap either. In many cases I think it is your own mindset, but also who is around you. That is not to say there is not some of an old boys' club still in our caucuses. But now, there's also support among the women.

I would say for women that feel they have a voice and want to be heard, politics is a great thing to do. Especially if you are at that point in your life where you can make it work and feel you can be effective. This is not a job that is out of reach for most people. All you have to do is be prepared to work, use a lot of common sense, and look in the best interests of the people you are representing. I think that most women can do this job. I think you have to go into it with a clear head and clear expectation of what it is going to take. At the end of the day there is no greater gift that you can give your community or your province than the service that you can provide. I think many times women undervalue themselves and undervalue their experiences and what their value can be. It sounds cliché to say that we are strong, but I think that our opportunities are without boundaries at this point in our lives.

---

[15] In 2019, the Nova Scotia Government passed the Human Organ and Tissue Donation Act, which legislated presumed consent for organ donation in the province. Under the Act, all adults in Nova Scotia are to be considered organ donors unless they opt out – a change from the previous system where an adult needed to opt in to be a donor.

Photo by Mosy Photography

38. The HONOURABLE SUZANNE LOHNES-CROFT
LIBERAL MLA FOR LUNENBURG 2013–PRESENT
Minister of Communities, Culture, and Heritage

I am from rural Nova Scotia, born and raised in Mahone Bay. I went away to Mount Saint Vincent University and took early childhood education, and then graduated and ended up teaching at the Child Studies Centre. In 1989 my husband had an opportunity with his position to move back to the South Shore, and I decided it was a good time [to go back]. So we returned, and I have remained here.

It has been great raising my family in rural Nova Scotia. My father was very involved in politics. He was a former mayor in Mahone Bay, and members of his family had filled council positions and positions of trustees in the town over. Our family history is in Mahone Bay. It was only natural for me to be involved in politics, community service, and volunteerism. I was initially going to run municipally, but Stephen McNeil came to me before I had done any nomination applications and asked me to run for the Liberals. I went for the nomination and it was not contested—I think that was a sign. Here I am. Two elections and I'm still here.

One of the questions I asked Stephen McNeil when I was considering being a possible nominee was about women. He said that women and their voices in caucus changed his whole perception of politics. He said the lens of women has changed the way he looks at policy and legislation, because the voices of women in the caucus have been so strong and consistent. That was my deciding factor.

I definitely think [women] have to work a lot harder to do well. And not just twice as hard, I think four times as hard, as men do. People make assumptions about you. Even getting the media to cover you is different. If a man was doing an announcement, all sorts of media would show up. If you do speeches in the legislature, the press does not pick it up. Sometimes they get up and walk out. I do not want to take away from the women who have made a path for us, but there's a long way still to go for equality.

Rural Nova Scotia is not always the loudest voice [in politics]. Everything is always bigger in HRM. I do honour and respect that our biggest tax base comes from HRM, but rural Nova Scotia is vital. People need services. I am not thinking about just today, I am thinking about the future of Nova Scotia as well. I think being a parent has changed everything about who I am, because I always look with the perspective of, 'How would I want my child to be treated in this situation? What do I want for my children in their future?' That perspective is really important in [politics]. A lot of my decision-making is not just about what is happening now, but it is how we are leaving this place. I really want to see Nova Scotia, especially rural Nova Scotia, left better because I am part of a government that moved forward, made tough decisions when tough decisions had to be made, and did not always make decisions because they were popular.

A remark that really resonated with me was that we are now seeing the last generation of true politicians because social media and opinion and negativity are going to prevent good people from offering up. It is very destructive, it is very intrusive. You are convicted by somebody's opinion on social media. It is a tough job. It is not meant for everybody. The bullying that goes on online can tear you down. But you cannot survive if you are letting [it] eat away at you. Not to say I have thick skin. I am thicker skinned than I once was, but I do not ever want to be so thick skinned that I do not feel empathy for people or stop listening to people. I think that is a really fine line in this job.

Getting involved in politics is not just being a politician. It is being a campaign manager. It is being an official agent. It is being a fundraiser for women. It is hard to fundraise in rural Nova Scotia if you are a woman. The donors are traditionally men. Often, you are relying on the old boys' club to write those cheques for your campaign, and it is a hard balance. Being a woman in politics, it is not always [being] the face of the party. It is all the people in the background. Start working on campaigns. Start coming out and listening to what goes on in the legislature. Watch what goes on in parliament on TV. Go to your local council meetings. Learn what it is like to door knock and defend yourself or promote yourself at the door. Politics is really about all those people behind you. Nailing in signs, knocking on doors, raising money. They are really important. Young women have to get involved at that level, so they have a better understanding.

Every experience, every opportunity, everything that was laid out for me, or by me, even my mistakes or successes in life all played a part in where I am today. If I was not raised by the parents that I had, if I did not have the childhood experiences, I might not be here. Everything that has happened in my life has led me to do this. I think everything happens for a reason in your life, whether it is for a lesson or to help you go further. I think things fall in place. You cannot succeed in everything, but you can learn from those mistakes.

Right before the submission of this book, Suzanne Lohnes-Croft was appointed to cabinet as Minister of Communities, Culture, and Heritage on October 13, 2020.

Photo by Mosy Photography

39. KARLA MACFARLANE
PC MLA FOR PICTOU WEST 2013–PRESENT
Interim Leader of the Opposition 2018–2018

My interest [in politics] began in junior high school being involved with student council, as [I was] the president. That led into senior high and being very involved in school activities. It was really a history teacher, Alan Gordon, who was actually Peter MacKay's first campaign manager, who always said to me, "You are definitely getting involved in politics." And I always [said], "No I'm not. I'm going to go be an actress." I was really interested in radio and television broadcasting—that's what I went to university for. You know, twenty years later or more, I guess my history teacher was right.

I always voted— that was a given. My parents would drag us if we ever said we weren't. But in my twenties and in my early thirties when my children, Chloe and Jack, were born, my priorities changed and I became more removed from the political realm. In my late thirties I got involved with my local PC Association in Pictou West. Over time, people kept suggesting, "You should run! You should run!"

One day, I finally felt my kids were old enough and the timing was right. But you have a lot of doubts. At the time, Charlie Parker had been our MLA for almost twelve years and was a cabinet minister with the NDP. I thought, *Oh my goodness. I have to take down a giant.* But the Liberal Party, the local Liberal Association of Pictou West, had called me, (even knowing my involvement with the local PC Association) and asked if I would consider running for them. I thought, *If they think I have a chance, maybe I really do.* So, we put our team together and we went for it.

I believe every day my gender is still recognized. Politics is still perhaps a man's realm. Every day, I feel there are pressures, but there are highlights as well. My goal has always been to ensure that everyone knows as females, we don't bring anything better to the table, but we bring something different and of equal value.

I do recall when I decided to put my name forward, a very strong Conservative man in his seventies, had come into my business that I owned in Pictou and said, "Karla, can I have a word with you?" At this point, I'm still considering putting my name forward to run for the nomination. I remember him coming in and he says, "Look, you're a great gal but there's no place for women in politics." That was definitely a turning point for me. Because I was like, "Watch me!" He really solidified that I was going to throw my name in the hat for the nomination.

I remember him saying, "Well, what do you know about fracking?" And I remember thinking that I wanted to ask him, *Well what do you know about women's rights?* It's interesting though, a year after I won and was elected as the MLA for Pictou West, he came into my constituency office with a dozen roses and apologized. I think that's a strong message that it is always best to take the high road and be graceful. Try to understand why they're coming from that angle or perspective. He is a great supporter now!

Being the only female [in caucus] was an interesting time.[16] I knew that I wanted to work extremely hard to ensure that the next election we would have [more] females running, and we did. I think for me, being the only female around the table was an opportunity to really show how hard I will work to have my voice heard. Because there were times at the table that I felt my voice was not being heard. There were times I felt I had to work twice as hard to have my voice heard. I did not slow down. I did not back away from that, and I did not do anything in haste.

I am a single mom. When I first started out, I had a ten year old and fourteen year old. They are seventeen and twenty-one now. It is challenging because [politics] is a job that I consider 24/7, and I feel that I put every effort forth to be accessible, but I am also responsible for running a household. I am lucky that my ex-husband is great, but you are still at the end of the day running a household by yourself. I always joked with the [men], I wasn't going home to where my groceries are bought, my banking is done, my driveway is shovelled and my clothes are washed. As a single mom in my position as an MLA it has been challenging to find that work/life balance.

Besides my children, one of my proudest moments was when my colleagues had voted me in to be interim leader. I was extremely humbled. That was a moment of disbelief because everything happened so quickly in the span of one day in our caucus office. It took me by surprise that they felt confident enough for me to lead them, and for me to lead them through a leadership race which was very difficult. Especially when you have three colleagues that were running against each other. That is a pretty moving moment for me to know they had that much faith in me.

---

[16] Karla was the only female member in the PC Caucus from 2013-2017.

Politics is fickle. Politics is a contact sport. No matter what, there is always going to be people throwing crap at you and it hurts at times. Even though I try not to engage in the negativity, I do take it home and I do get very analytical about it and I wonder, *Why? Why did they say that? Why do they think that?* You sometimes start to lose faith in what you are doing, but I always remind myself that I will never compromise my integrity and to trust my gut. When something like my colleagues supported me in being a leader, or perhaps getting an award for something, or simply being recognized for a piece of legislation I may have introduced, it injects you again with that reason why you are doing this. And in my case, it is [because] people are my passion. They always have been my passion and this job allows my passion to meet purpose, which is helping people.

Photo courtesy of Pam Eyking

40. PAM EYKING
LIBERAL MLA FOR VICTORIA-THE LAKES 2013–2017

Ariel Gough gave a TED Talk called "Unlikely" that really struck home with me. She spent a month with females from her community to empower them, but what she learned is that they were already empowered. I could identify with the women she had interviewed, and it suddenly struck me that I was somewhat of an 'unlikely.' This in turn helped me identify with other empowered women and left a lasting impression on me.

I grew up in Dartmouth, the only girl, and middle child to two brothers. As a child and throughout my teenage years, I loved my motorbike and my target practice. I preferred to be in nature and enjoyed helping my dad with home repairs and with building projects. I had some great teachers that brought out my strengths, but I was directed toward the trades because of the obstacles my Dyslexia presented. I earned my trade as a hairstylist when I was eighteen, and was working in Dartmouth when I met my husband, Mark.

Engaged at nineteen and married at twenty, I moved to Cape Breton with Mark where we began a family business in farming. This was very different from what I was accustomed to in Dartmouth. The isolation was hard and communication was limited due to our location and the technology at the time. Though isolated physically, I suddenly had less privacy by way of communication. We had a party line—a phone line you shared with neighbours and it suddenly cost money to call home because of the distance. It was an adjustment not being able to talk with friends and family as frequently as I had in the past and this was stressful at times because life was moving fast. I had my first baby a year after we married (we had four children over nine years) and at the same time we had a growing farm enterprise. I enjoyed developing the marketing and promotional branch of the business and eventually took over the books. I learned a lot about business during this time.

Back then, the farming industry was largely male dominated. I never considered that being a female could create barriers or obstacles, or even that owning a business and raising a family could be separated. Both filled my days for the next twenty years. I learned to be flexible, resilient, and resourceful. Neither Mark or I were involved in politics at this time. We weren't even members of a particular political party.

Before politics, we had done some work in Panama helping to erect their first greenhouses. I realized I enjoy working on large projects. We went back to Panama a few years later to find they expanded. They had built almost a hundred greenhouses in total. The first person to build one was a woman. She endured quite a bit of criticism for that bold move. People told her she was crazy. When we visited her years later and saw the amount of growth, she said, "Now everyone is crazy!"

When Mark was approached to run in 2000, I worked both behind the scenes and alongside him.[17] I accompanied him during and after the campaign and on subsequent campaigns in the future. Time was precious and limited. Political events were opportunities for us to be together. Of course, we talked intimately about everything going on in our lives including politics. During those years I learned a lot about the role of a politician and what political life looked like for an individual and their family.

Premier Stephen McNeil planted the seed for me to run as an MLA several years before it happened. I had four children at home that I was still raising, so I really didn't think much of it at the time. Not until someone from the Liberal Party approached me to run for MLA in 2013 did I give it serious consideration. By this time the kids were all independent. Mark was still an MP and we realized if I became an MLA, it would give us a very unique opportunity to collaborate on local projects. Together we were able to allocate a lot of money for infrastructure and tourism projects in our area which still gives me a sense of pride today.

Everyone's experience in politics is different but I do think women bring unique skills and perspectives that complement the traditional political standard men have set. Women I have worked with seemed to have particular strengths in multi-tasking and working collaboratively. They are also deeply empathetic which helps to understand another's motivation when sitting down at the negotiating table.

I accredit a large part of my success to other women in the Liberal family that supported me. I was very lucky to sit in a caucus with wonderful, strong women, and I'd be remiss to ignore that we had a lot of support from our male colleagues too. I believe the premier set the tone for such an inclusive work environment and that fostered productivity. Gender is a factor of diversity and experience, but even more important is the individual character and capability of those colleagues. I was lucky to have been surrounded by a team of very capable people of outstanding character.

---

[17] Pam's husband Mark Eyking served as the Liberal Member of Parliament for Sydney-Victoria from 2009-2019.

During my time as an MLA, I made a lot of good friends with some highly respected, hardworking women who were very good at tackling issues from many different angles. Diana Whalen was a very dedicated MLA and minister. Karen Casey was strong, reliable, and always gave me sage advice. Joyce Treen was one of the most passionate MLAs I had the pleasure of working with. Margaret Miller was grounded and helped me get my bearings at times I felt lost. These are just some of the many remarkable people I worked with and alongside.

When I think back, I was unaware that I was an 'unlikely' and maybe that was one of the underlying factors to my success. It never occurred to me that I could not achieve what I was setting out to achieve. Instead, I focused on my strengths to the best of my abilities. Like everyone, I questioned my own resolve and abilities at times, but self-doubt never prevented me from doing my best. I just put my head down and got the work done.

What I've learned from past experiences is not to let anything stop you. We need diversity in politics. We need people who have struggled in the education system to be involved because they have intimate knowledge on how to improve it. We need people from all walks of life, who can represent all the people in our society. We are a variety of people and we need a variety of people to represent us. If you have a passion for politics then go for it.

Take risks in life. I moved to Cape Breton, built a business, and grew a family. I helped my husband in his political career and then had my own. It was not always easy. The premier took fiscal responsibility very seriously and we took a lot of hits for that. Today I don't think about the hits, but of how proud I am to have been an active force of change at that time for Nova Scotia.

You do not have to be an elected official to make change. There are lots of ways to help move good policy along. The most important thing is possessing the passion to create change. I fell in love with Cape Breton on a camping trip with my parents as a teen. That love transferred to passion which I used as a driving force throughout my life—from family, to business, to politics.

At the end of the day, I'm very proud and grateful to have had the chance to represent the home I love.

I truly am blessed.

41. MARIAN MANCINI
NDP MLA FOR DARTMOUTH SOUTH 2015–2017

Marian Mancini became the MLA of Dartmouth South in 2015 in a by-election. She did not reoffer in 2017.

Marian was raised in Glace Bay, Nova Scotia. She had a successful career as a lawyer in legal aid. She served as provincial party president of the NDP from 1999–2001. Her husband, Peter Mancini served as MP for Sydney-Victoria from 1997–2000. She moved to Dartmouth in 2001 alongside her husband and three children.

She did not participate in this book.[18]

---

[18] This information was adapted from Nancy King, "Glace Bay native squeaks out win in Dartmouth South" (Cape Breton Post, 2015).

Photo by Mosy Photography

42. LISA ROBERTS
NDP MLA FOR HALIFAX NEEDHAM 2016- PRESENT

I was always interested in politics. I watched and discussed politics with my dad, but I did not consider running until I was over forty. I studied international development and development economics, and worked some in non-profits and international development, but I was mostly a journalist. I had a career of about fifteen years in journalism, with a lot of freelance and casual employment, and then five years at *Information Morning* at CBC Radio in Halifax. Being a journalist is another way of following public policy conversations, and I always really admired different individuals who were playing leadership roles or who were just showing leadership from whatever role they were in.

I think at some point, after I had my kids and when I was at a point in my life where I was personally grounded, it dawned on me that I didn't just admire those people I was watching, I wanted to be like those people. Jennifer Watts and Megan Leslie are two women in particular who I really looked up to—and look up to still—and I was able to get to know and learn directly from them. I initially did the Campaign School for Women in 2011, because I was so inspired by Jennifer Watts that I wanted to run for council in 2012. Then the boundaries of the electoral districts were redrawn and I ended up in the same district as her, so I became her campaign manager. I feel like that was a huge gift to me because by supporting her, I learned a ton and met a lot of people that led to other work that I did afterward.

Being directly involved in a municipal election campaign was the beginning of my transition out of journalism. That municipal campaign led to my involvement in some community organizing and in 2015, I became executive director of a community non-profit organization. When Maureen MacDonald resigned in 2016, and I was asked to seek the nomination for the NDP, I felt really ready.

From 2012 to 2015, I was represented municipally by Jennifer Watts, provincially by Maureen MacDonald, and federally by Megan Leslie. As a progressive woman with a lot of concerns around climate change, but also equity and women's rights and our future as a society, it made a big difference to me that I felt represented. I particularly think about it now because I'm in opposition, and I'm in the third party. I want very much to have more direct access to the levers of government. But at no point did I feel poorly represented by Megan Leslie because she wasn't in government. It made a huge difference to me that she was there.

Having kids actually is part of what enables me to do this job. Being in a relationship with my kids has emotionally grounded me in a way that I wasn't grounded in my twenties and thirties. I was much less focused than I am now. Also having the time, particularly during my first maternity leave, to really turn off social media and read a lot of books about social change was very productive for me. I came out of it ready to do something new. It was like a new era.

When I was first elected and my kids were six and eight, there were tears when I did not get home to do cuddles. That was really hard. But I mostly feel like having them in my life allows me to do a really good check with myself about how I'm doing the job. When I am with them, even if that time is not always as much as I would like, I try to be really present with them. If stuff is intruding on that time with me mentally, then I know I have to make some adjustments. I have to say that my partner is a very active, engaged father. Also my parents moved to Halifax from Newfoundland in 2012 and they've been very helpful, especially during intense periods like election campaigns.

What am I proud of? This is pretty modest, but I'm proud that I take the bus to the Legislature. I am proud that I ride my bike. I am proud that if I can't do either of those, I use CarShare. I am trying to reduce my environmental footprint, but the way I move through my constituency also allows me to witness people's lives and their struggles. I am not trying to distance myself from the challenges people are engaged in. I am also proud that at my constituency office, we treat people with a lot of respect when they come to us for help. People feel like they are heard. We cannot always get them the answers or tangible things they want from the provincial government, but I feel like they consistently have an experience of feeling respected and welcomed in my office, and I am proud of that. Finally, I have had some success in advocating for particular causes or projects with government. A school playground that badly needed investment got that attention. I have had some success and impact in supporting the ALS Society of Nova Scotia and New Brunswick. And at the level of my constituency office, we're always working to direct support to non-profit organizations based in Halifax Needham working in the areas of housing, mental health, food security and the arts.

My advice to young women is do not be afraid to help. A lot of young people are wanting to make a mark, [which is] great and I understand wanting to self-actualize. But sometimes there is so much to gain by helping somebody else first, and working on their project. You get to do all of the learning and make the connections. Certainly, I evolved by helping others. If you aren't exactly sure what you want to do, or how to do it, there is always a way—particularly with political parties—to show up and help. And sometimes the biggest hurdle to overcome is just convincing yourself that you should walk through the door and pick up the phone and make that offer. I think a lot of people think, *oh it's not my place, I've never done that before, I don't know anyone who has ever done that.* If you can make the call or walk into a campaign office, you'll be put to work and you will learn a ton. You will be more comfortable making the next step.

One other thing I say fairly often is that sometimes people disparage politics by saying it's just theatre and nothing gets decided in the legislature. And I have come to think that, in fact, theatre is pretty powerful. By saying things out loud we change the world that we live in. I have tried very hard in the legislature to speak from a genuine, authentic place. Whether it is about the need to rise to the challenge of climate change and to be ambitious in our response, or whether it is speaking about some of the structural inequities in Nova Scotia that go back to how this province was settled and how African Nova Scotians were marginalized and Mi'kmaq people were colonized…. No matter what it is, I try to speak from a genuine place and with an openness to connecting with other MLAs. I am proud that, not all the time but with relative frequency, I feel that I have the attention of the legislature. The room gets quiet and sometimes MLAs from other parties will say something to me after about what I said. It is hard to know what impact that has, but I feel like it has an impact. I feel like it matters.

Photo by Mosy Photography

43. TAMMY MARTIN
NDP MLA FOR CAPE BRETON CENTRE 2017–2020

Initially, I worked in healthcare and I became very active in my union. After that, I took a lot of union education and became the president of my local [union] for years. From there, I became a national representative with Canadian Union of Public Employees. I saw running for MLA as the next step in the evolution of my career. Union leadership and politics are very connected and they are very, very similar.

Funny enough, there was always an unwritten or unspoken notion that when my predecessor retired, I would probably be the one to take his place—although that was never said out loud. One day I was driving to work and an announcement came on the radio that he had retired that morning and my stomach sank. I thought, *Oh wow. I don't know if I'm ready.* Then the phone call came.

[Public office] has been difficult. I cannot say that it has been a breeze, because it has not. I was a single mom, which meant I was on the road a lot [away] from my daughter. In hindsight when I look back at that, it only helped her become the woman that she is today. To see that anything is possible, you can do whatever you set your mind to. I do not want to say that there are challenges because we are women, but there are. I do not give into the fact that I either do not get something or get something because I am a woman. I do not buy into that. But at the end of the day, there are certain things that you just cannot avoid, like childcare, and housekeeping. As a single mom, that was my personality—and I am sure as many of colleagues will say, a big part of that falls on a woman's shoulders.

My biggest advice would be just go for it. Like I said, there are challenges. I remember some union sisters used to exchange ideas on how to make going away a little bit easier. I used to stick a note in my daughter's lunch or on her bed that would just tell her why I am away and what I am doing—which she knew. And now, when I went away and took a union job in Manitoba for a short time, she stuck a note in my suitcase, which said basically everything I've said to her over her life.

My daughter [is] my greatest challenge and my biggest accomplishment. It's been her and me for her whole life. It is hard but you have to show them that there is a path and that you can do whatever you set your mind to. She is an emergency room nurse now and at the end of every day or week I just reminded her that she can do whatever she puts her mind to, and not to let anyone ever tell you that you can't.

It does not matter if you are a woman, if you are of a different race or colour. You can do whatever you set your mind to. You just have to believe in yourself. Even when you do not, you have to believe you can do it.

44. ALANA PAON
INDEPENDENT MLA FOR CAPE BRETON-RICHMOND 2017–PRESENT

Alana Paon was elected MLA of Cape Breton-Richmond in May 2017. She grew up in Isle Madame as the youngest of five children. She moved to Halifax at nineteen where she raised her son, Gharrett.

Alana had a career in consulting, specializing in areas such as community economic development and youth leadership. Later in her career she also owned and operated a sheep farm in Antigonish County.

She did not participate in this book.[19]

---

[19] This information was adapted from Marjorie Simmins, "Straight off the farm" (Halifax Magazine, 2017).

Photo by Mosy Photography

45. RAFAH DICOSTANZO
MLA FOR CLAYTON PARK WEST 2017–PRESENT

I came to Canada in 1984 as a student. I also immigrated because of the war that was happening in my home country of Iraq. Through my educational journey, I ended up in Canada; I had come alone at the time. My family followed two years later and settled in Ontario.

Growing up as a Christian in Iraq, I was aware that we had no freedom of speech, especially regarding politics. Also, there were no politicians in my family to look up to, as it was dangerous for Christians to get involved. If you had told me then that I would someday become a politician, I would have never believed you.

Back in 2003–2004, when former Prime Minister Jean Chrétien stood up to former U.S. President George Bush to say that Canada would not join in bombing Iraq, I thought, *Wow, they are doing the right thing. Who is making these decisions?* That is when my intrigue in politics arose and I wanted to help. My husband, who had graduated law school with Geoff [Regan], advised me to help out with [Geoff's] election that was on the horizon.

My political knowledge at the time was very limited; I did not even know what 'constituent' or 'riding' meant, or that we had three levels of government. I started delivering flyers, then got a bit of courage and started phoning people during campaigns. During that time, I was also introduced to former MLA of Clayton Park West, Diana Whalen, with whom I helped in her campaign and enjoyed knocking on doors for the provincial election. I then joined both the federal and provincial [Liberal] boards in my riding. I truly enjoyed that learning experience.

Working as a medical interpreter for twenty years, I have always seen myself as an effective connector for newcomers because I understand Canadian culture, and the wonderful social system that we enjoy in this country. I made it my mandate to help newcomers, in particular women, of how they can open the doors for their daughters to enjoy and to benefit from our rights in Canada.

I am blessed to have raised two daughters the Canadian way. I don't think they understand what their circumstances would have been like if they were born and raised in a different country. Canada has afforded them freedom of speech, and many opportunities in sports and in academics. Most importantly, my daughters chose their careers without restrictions, and can love whoever they choose to love.

I love my riding of Clayton Park West, where I have resided for thirty-five years, because it is the most diverse, and most dense, riding. I continually try to show the newcomers how different and positive politics is in Canada. I am very proud of all that I have accomplished in just two short years, and I believe I have made notable strides, particularly in binding multiculturalism with politics in my riding.

46. BARBARA ADAMS
PC MLA FOR COLE HARBOUR-EASTERN PASSAGE 2017–PRESENT

My father, Jack Hare, was my hero, my teacher, and the person who instilled in me the value of civic engagement and constant curiosity. My dad served as the executive director for the Health Services and Insurance Commission for Nova Scotia until his retirement in 1987. His retirement, although I did not know it at the time, signalled the end of an era for me. The end of overlooking the legislature with him through his office window next door while we debated the issues of the day, long before I even knew what 'government' was.

Debating with dad prepared me for my own chance to participate in a mock parliament when I was in high school, where I stood in the Nova Scotia Legislature and learned that indeed, women could and needed to be part of this political world, a foreshadowing of what was to come for me.

While studying physiotherapy at Dalhousie University from 1980 to 1984, I joined the Youth Progressive Conservative Association and my first political event was Joe Clark's Leadership Review. I quickly realized that many political decisions are decided long before a convention.

As an adult I began noticing the impact that government decisions had on my daily life and I knew it was time to become more engaged. Initially, I volunteered with a number of organizations and then served on various boards of directors like CARP Nova Scotia & VON Halifax.

As a clinical researcher and allied health professional with a certificate in business management, I had twenty-five years of hospital experience and ten years in private practice. In addition to running a chronic pain program at the Atlantic Balance and Dizziness Centre in Dartmouth for ten years, I was simultaneously the clinical director of PhysioCare at Home, a Halifax-based home care physiotherapy and occupational therapy company. This provided me with the opportunity to work in home care and long-term care. Later, being appointed the critic for Seniors, Home Care and Long-Term Care as an MLA was a natural fit.

Over many years, I wrote a 400-page book called the *Fibromyalgia (FM) and Chronic Pain Owner's Manual*. I wrote this book based on my personal experience with FM as well as my research and clinical care. I am a guest speaker for the Arthritis Society and the Alzheimer's Society of NS and have given hundreds of free talks to health profession students, physicians, seniors' groups, and other organizations Being a good public speaker is essential to the work we do in the Nova Scotia Legislature.

I eagerly shared my knowledge and ideas for change with government and influential stakeholders but quickly learned that the 'power' to change legislation and health regulations was inside the legislature. I decided I had to make a difference, and to do that, I would become one of the people who had direct input into the legislative system. I was almost ready to run.

When I reviewed the background of the Nova Scotia MLAs in power in 2016, there were only three healthcare professionals. Given that healthcare takes up nearly half of the provincial budget, it did not make sense to me that out of fifty-one MLAs, only three had ever worked in healthcare. I wondered if having a healthcare background, a commitment to making change, and a big voice would be a good combination for the role of a provincial politician.

I believed then, as I do even more now, that if we want better healthcare in Nova Scotia, we need more healthcare professionals in the legislature. In 2017, with my two sons, Dr. Chris Lavoie and Corporal John Lavoie, and two stepsons, Mike and Ryan Adams, grown up and moved out west, I knew it was my time to make change from the inside.

Volunteering is something I have done my entire life and will always do as a community-minded person. Volunteering became the way I entered the PC Party. I stood for the constituency of Cole Harbour–Eastern Passage in the 2017 provincial election. We made history that year as all four candidates in my constituency were women—a first for Nova Scotia. My team worked hard, I worked hard, and the people of my community trusted me to represent them in the House of Assembly, a privilege I am so honoured to hold.

The experience over the past three years has been both thrilling and frustrating. It is a journey into a world that only fifty women in Nova Scotia have had the privilege to participate in…for now!

In my career as a healthcare professional, I was used to working in a world that was predominantly female. I did not face barriers of being treated differently nor was I viewed as less than because I was a woman. Being a woman was an advantage because we are traditionally viewed as caring, honest, and empathetic. These traits are still a huge advantage in the political world but perhaps are not viewed as such. Power appears to be the coveted trait and to this day, **male politicians are still often viewed as having more knowledge, more experience, and therefore more power.**

There are times when I walk into a meeting with male MLAs, and those in the room will greet or shake hands with the male MLAs and assume I am the assistant. It is quite simply something that I am aware o—but it doesn't stop me from doing what I need to do. It just makes me work a little harder to ensure I stand in my place and make my voice heard. I am more than comfortable doing that. I want to be sure that my granddaughters are inspired to follow in my footsteps should they have that dream as well.

I do not know where I heard this advice from, but I have followed it my whole life. If you are not sure what you want to do with your life, ask yourself what frustrates you the most and then find a career that helps you solve whatever that frustration is.

My mother, Marjorie Hare, continues to promote the value of volunteerism even as she celebrates her ninetieth birthday. As a teenager I volunteered with a unique program for children with special needs called the 'Upward Bound Program' at the YMCA in Dartmouth. This program was offered at a time when these precious children were not as integrated into society as they are today. It saddened me no end that these children did not have the same opportunities I had purely because they were born with a physical or intellectual disability. When I was four years old, I temporarily lost the ability to walk for two weeks. I was hospitalized and terrified that I was never going to go home or walk again. That experience left a lasting impression on me.

The joy that I got from working with these children lasted a lifetime. It instilled a deep sense of gratitude for my own health and compassion for helping others overcome hardship. This became a lifelong vocation.

It's no coincidence that I became a physiotherapist and that my focus as a politician deals directly with healthcare. I have devoted my entire career to helping patients, families, and organizations assess, diagnose, and plan strategies to overcome obstacles. Working in politics requires the same set of people skills, strategic planning and the powerful desire to look for new opportunities for growth and innovation.

An important message I want girls to hear from me is that you do not have to be an extrovert or outgoing to be in politics. From a very young age I was incredibly shy. I was nervous in social settings and I still am, but I have learned skills to manage it. It is a barrier that can be overcome.

What I learned through the last four decades is that you develop many useful skills over the years. You will not know exactly how to do a job until you are doing it. You prepare the best you can and surround yourself with positive thinkers who can challenge you, guide you, and support you when you fall. In the winter of 2018, I fulfilled a life-long yearning to help out on a medical mission. I travelled over my holidays to a small village called Lokpo, in the country of the Republic of Benin, Africa. This experience changed my life. The amazing spirit of the people we worked for and with has left a lasting impression on my heart.

If you are passionate about an issue, you want to align yourself with others who have a similar view as there is strength in numbers. You have to be willing to listen to others who have new information or a different life experience than you. This is very important. The ability to keep an open mind is probably one of the hardest and most important skills. When you feel like you disagree, lean in closer to learn more.

I never dreamed when I was a little girl that I would be where I am today. Sometimes I still pinch myself when I walk into the legislature. I look around the chamber where I did model parliament when I was fifteen years old, and marvel that forty-two years later I am standing in the same place as all those years ago.

You never know where you are going to go in life, but if you have a desire to go there, then you have got to go for it. You will never regret trying, no matter what the outcome.

Photo by Mosy Photography

47. ELIZABETH SMITH-McCROSSIN
PC MLA FOR CUMBERLAND NORTH 2017–PRESENT

I was always involved in student government. I remember when I was sixteen, seeing the results of what I think was a municipal election come in. I distinctly remember looking at a newspaper article, and there were eight white men probably over the age of seventy that all won. That really stood out to me visually. I thought, *There's something wrong with this.* Fifty percent of our population is female, yet if we looked at the people who are governing municipal, provincial, federal [governments]…predominantly, it is men. I just think our governing bodies should reflect the population through diversity and gender. We need to work hard on that. So right from the beginning, from that age, I was aware of it.

I have an older sister, and my mom passed away when I was five, so she was kind of a mother figure in my life. She found a letter that I had sent her when I was sixteen after this [municipal] election that said, "This is wrong! We need more women in politics!" So that was my first real passion. I have always been interested. When I see a problem or a change, I always think that we need to look for a solution. I think as a legislator, that's where you can work on finding solutions.

We face [sexism] just about every day. Just yesterday, we were in a meeting, and the presenter acknowledged one of the men that [ran] in the leadership race last year but did not acknowledge me.[20]

---

[20] Elizabeth ran for the leadership of the Progressive Conservative Party in 2018.

Maybe it had nothing to do with the fact that I was a woman, but you cannot help but feel that it is gender related. I never let that be a barrier. It just makes me more determined to be strong, not just for me but for other women.

Well, if I thought about my legacy—if I die today, what have I left behind? I think I'm probably like any mother; my greatest legacy is my children. I know that probably sounds corny and a typical answer, but it is the truth. That is my greatest legacy, and that is my greatest hope for the future. We all work, but our greatest hope for the future is our next generation. You hope that the world will become a better place than it is today. I think probably any generation wants that for the next. My husband and I have four children— a daughter and three sons. My son had cancer when he was sixteen. I just look at him and I am so thankful. I can do a lot of interesting things in life, but they will always be my greatest legacy.

My best advice is that if you feel that calling—because I do believe it is a calling—then listen to your heart and go with it. Not everybody has that placed on their heart. I believe if you have that desire and you are being pulled in that direction, there is a reason for that. Listen to your intuition, listen to your heart. The women that have come before us have paved the way so we have more doors open to us, and we can make our choices, but it doesn't mean we can be everything to everyone all the time. I think that's one of the hardest lessons I've had to learn, because I want to do everything and be everything to everyone all the time.

When you make a choice to go in one direction it means that maybe you can't do something else. I chose to wait to try to get into elected office once my children were grown. Living in rural Nova Scotia, if you are elected to office, you cannot go home every night to your children and to your family. I was not willing to sacrifice that for political life. Now that my children are grown, I'm not sacrificing that. In fact, three out of four of my children live here in the city.

As far as my story, I feel very strongly that we can be doing much better with our healthcare system. In Canada, we have a publicly-funded healthcare system and there's been a lot of changes over the years with regards to pharmaceuticals, the way medicine has changed with technology and diagnostics. We have not necessarily been managing our healthcare system in step with the changes. My mom passed away when I was five, so I've always been drawn to [healthcare]. Growing up knowing that my mom was only twenty-eight when she passed away of skin cancer and was able to have what she needed—it is very important to me that other people also have what they need.

I wanted to be a nurse from a young age, and as a nurse, I always wanted things to be better. I always felt like we need to be improving our healthcare system. I started four different businesses all with a focus on health. I had a local organic food store, focusing on healthy eating and nutrition. I had a holistic health centre, a collaborative health centre, and I had a nutrition counselling business. My passion is healthcare and caring for people, making sure that people get access to services when they need them, which comes from a place of authenticity.

You have to remember what your goal is, what you are trying to achieve, and then when you are going through the valleys or the challenging moments, you keep your eye on that goal. Never lose sight of that.

Photo by Mosy Photography

48. SUSAN LEBLANC
NDP MLA FOR DARTMOUTH NORTH 2017–PRESENT

My background is in theatre. I studied to become an actor and was a performer for many years. I also helped run an ensemble theatre company and taught a lot of theatre. I was engaged at Dalhousie with young artists for a long time, directing them or teaching them theatre or acting.

There are a lot of things that come into play when someone decides to run, and for me it was that I felt at a point in my theatre career where I was not doing enough politically or for social justice with my work. I loved my work and I love what my company does, but I felt this pull for me to do more and I could not figure out how to do it in theatre. I was [becoming] more aware of the labour movement and different social justice struggles, and the intersectionality of all those different struggles. I started paying more attention to politics, and volunteering on campaigns. When my family moved to Dartmouth North, it was clear that the NDP, which was always the party that I was involved with, might need a candidate for the next election. I did a lot of, for lack of a less cheesy term, 'soul-searching' about it all. Then I just decided to do it and put my name forward.

I was very torn about leaving my theatre company. Our company was built by three or four of us together for almost twenty years. It was part of who I was, and it still is. It was not until I had the conversation with one of my co-artistic directors, who is also one of my best friends, that [I decided]. I needed to know for sure that it was going to be okay if I left, that I could come back someday, or that we would still be able to have a relationship. I wondered what it meant for who I was if I stopped doing theatre. This, of course, was way after all of the discussions with my partner, making sure it would be okay for our family. The discussions with my colleagues was the final thing that allowed me to accept that I wanted to do it.

When I ran, the candidates from the other main parties—the Liberals and the PCs—were women. That was kind of interesting. I was elected at the cusp of a change. It was at the beginning of the Me Too movement, and in our first legislative sitting in 2017 on the Day of the Girl, I did a member's statement. It was just as the story of Harvey Weinstein was breaking in LA, it really was not in the mainstream media yet. In my member's statement I said I couldn't celebrate the Day of the Girl right now because all of these different things were happening. I refused to say, "Everything is so great for women!" We're still working in a heavily patriarchal, European, colonial system which is something I acknowledge every day.

I have two small kids, and I'm raising them to be politically aware and to ask questions about topics like fairness and justice. We have taken both of them on marches, protests, and rallies since they were infants. I hope that continues. I am proud of the theatre I made. In politics, I think I'm most proud of having a strong voice to speak about issues in my community, but also larger issues of injustice; being able to recognize that the issues I work on may not be my struggles, but they are struggles of so many. And to be able to amplify community voices and be able to pay attention to what's going on in my community, in the province, and in the world.

To be able to call for change by amplifying the voices that are calling for the change.

I think people have to go into politics for the right reasons, but those reasons will be different for everybody. I think that if someone is considering that, they have to look deeply inward and see why they want to do it, and if they can achieve something by doing it. It is not an easy job. The one thing I find exhausting about it is that the minute you are elected, you are accountable to thousands of people who may or may not agree with you, may or may not think you are doing a good job, and demand that you must be working all of the time. That's hard. It is hard to know that pressure is out there. Especially when you have a family. Part of the thing that sets me apart—although not in our caucus—is that I have little kids. I am a mother of little kids and at the time when I got elected, they were in daycare. That is a particular place to come from and there is a pressure on you with kids that age. I try to be true to that too and represent from that point of view.

I feel like the other part of my job is to represent where I come from in the legislature, and that is art. I try to amplify artists and the struggle of artists, but also to honour the work of artists in the legislature. I remember I started doing member's statements about things going on in the community, but I would devote some of mine to a theatre show opening or a work of art. Yesterday I did one about Nocturne and I identified the pieces I saw. It's really important to me to be able [to tell] the greater community and politicians the benefit and necessity of the arts.

Photo by Mosy Photography

49. CLAUDIA CHENDER
NDP MLA FOR DARTMOUTH SOUTH 2017–PRESENT

My background is in law, which is part of how I came to this role. My constitutional law professor and mentor at law school was a former attorney general. He had been an MLA and cabinet minister, and he asked us one day when we were in class, "How many of you want to be a politician?" Nobody raised their hands. And then he chastised us by saying, "Listen, I know you might think politics is dirty, but you guys are studying, you are smart, you understand legislation and law. At least some of you have to be willing to take on that public service." And that really stuck with me as something I thought maybe I would do. Then there came a point in my life where I was sort of at a crossroads, trying to figure out what my next steps were and the stars aligned. I love and am really connected with my community, and my MLA resigned somewhat unexpectedly.

As I was contemplating a run for office, my now-colleague Susan Leblanc had just won the NDP nomination contest in Dartmouth North. I knew Sue a little bit so I went out to coffee with her. I said, "Talk to me about this. How did you make your choice? What was the nomination like? I want to know everything." I became convinced through that conversation that if she could do it, I could do it too. I knew that my community wanted to continue to have representation that reflected them, and I felt that I could add something. I guess the rest is history.

I think the whole way in which the political system is structured, but also the way in which our society is structured, is still very patriarchal and very oriented towards a male norm. We battle that on a structural level inside the legislature. I'm the House leader for the NDP, so I am the first line in our party for figuring out how legislation moves through the House, and I'm in the discussions on when we sit, how long we sit, those kinds of things. I think I bring a different eye to that in terms of the boundaries and schedules, and a sense that in order to be good legislators we need to be good humans too. We need to live lives that allow us to do that.

There are a lot of ways that things have always been done that rely on the physical labour of spouses and partners. If you listen to the Springtide *Off Script* podcast, which consists of exit interviews with MLAs, a lot of the older men will say things like, "I didn't need a constituency assistant! My wife answered the phone, and my daughter took messages!" And they do not realize that the reason they did not need a constituency assistant is because they had drafted all the women in their life into that role. I think for most of the women currently sitting, it is just us, or some of us have partners who work full time, too. I do not have the luxury of a 'wife'—and not many people do. I do not think that is yet reflected in how we do business.

I would add, I think there are a lot of men in the legislature who have young children, too. They are also experiencing changing gender norms, and we hear a lot about how they struggle to find time to be supportive partners and be with their families. I think we need a shift inside the legislature, and I run up against that in how I have experienced the legislature as a woman.

But on a really personal level, I think my strategy of how to show up in this role has been to just be as authentic as I can, and as true to what is good for me, what is good for my family and what is good for women. I try to shift the things around me by doing what I feel needs to be done, on a constituency level, a political level, and a personal level, without acquiescing to the way the system works. So far that has worked more or less.

I think the situation in our caucus is very unusual. Four of us [out of five] are women, and a lot of our staff are women. We all have children. Four of us have young children. From a caucus perspective, I am really grateful to be in an environment where there is a basic understanding of all of the balls in the air that women are often juggling, especially mothers. I feel really well supported from that perspective. I am proud to be a part of this team because we are doing things differently. An almost all-female caucus doesn't exist anywhere else in North America, as far as we know. We are consistently advocating for positions that I feel good about that I think are unapologetically progressive.

We have had successes in that regard, most recently with the passage of a bill I introduced mandating 'bubble zones' around reproductive health facilities.[21] This is to prevent people who are accessing these services, abortion in particular, from intimidation and to protect the safety of patients and healthcare providers. The passage of this bill as a first-term opposition MLA has certainly been a highlight of my job to date, and we saw a genuine coalescing in the legislative chamber as MLAs from all parties spoke clearly, and at times emotionally, in support of this bill.

---

[21] Bill 242, the Protecting Access to Reproductive Health Care Act was passed with unanimous consent of the Legislature and received Royal Assent on March 10, 2020.

Our caucus was also instrumental in getting maternity leave extended to municipal counsellors and MLAs. Similarly, eliminating the waiting period to be able to take maternity leave in the labour standards code, so that women who have just started a job are not under some kind of probation. We've really started to move the needle on some good, strong, feminist policy. I think that is really important to make space for women to show up and be leaders. What we see across the board—we see it in law, in politics, in business, and on boards, is that there is no shortage of brilliant women, and no shortage of brilliant educated women, but we still are in a situation where there are a ton at the bottom and very few at the top. Now I think it is about trying to clear that path so that there aren't obstacles to women achieving success.

Photo by Mosy Photography

50. KIM MASLAND
PC MLA FOR QUEENS-SHELBURNE 2017–PRESENT

I worked for a member of Parliament, Gerald Keddy, for over eighteen years as his executive assistant and chief of staff, so I was well-versed in the world of politics before I decided to offer my name for the ballot. When Mr. Keddy retired in 2015, I was left with a real feeling that I needed a purpose and a job that would continue to fulfill that purpose. The idea that people need to take care of one another had underpinned my entire career; in fact it has driven my entire life. My time at Mr. Keddy's office showed me the impact an elected representative can actually have on people's lives—and I am not talking about the big things, I am talking about the daily struggles people are facing while sitting in front of your desk looking for help and direction. I needed a job that would continue to fulfill my need to serve the public.

I was fortunate to receive a position with the Queens County Senior Safety Program, working at the Queens RCMP detachment. As the senior safety coordinator, I quickly learned of the lack of services available to help seniors, and of the complexity of navigating the services that did exist. I would receive calls all hours of the day and night which required visits, at times with RCMP officers, to help calm seniors, frightened because of their living conditions. I worked to provide services and education for seniors so that they could remain safe and independent in their homes. This position opened my eyes to things I had never realized were happening all around me in my community.

One day that shook me to my very core was a call asking for a wellbeing check. What I was about to walk into was something I will never forget. The house was in poor repair, isolated, cold, full of black mold and the odours of that day still remain with me. I was presented with a widowed senior, living alone, frightened, cold, very ill, and uncared for. Bills were lying unpaid on the table and groceries in the fridge had been expired for six months. I sat on the floor and held the shaking, swollen hand of this senior, and thought, *how is this happening?* I still drive by this house every day.

It took hours of sitting on the floor and listening to memories, building a relationship of trust so that I could call for help. The fear of the senior was, "If I leave my home for medical help and care, I will never return." Finally, the ambulance arrived, and I traveled to the hospital to help reduce the anxiety and uncertainty. The last time I held that hand was when the client said, "Thank you, I think I am in the right place and I am doing the right thing. I never would have done this without you. I have nobody."

I visited the next day and I was so happy to see a smile, to chat, and to know my client was safe, clean, warm, and not hungry. The next time I returned to the hospital, I was advised my client passed away in the middle of the night—peacefully. That day, walking from the hospital I was overcome with emotion thinking, *if only I could have gotten there sooner, how do I change this?* Although running for public office was always something I had thought about, even dreamed about doing, it was that day that I felt the urgency and need to put my name on a ballot. I was deeply disturbed by the thought of how many others may be suffering in silence that we don't know about. I kept thinking, *how does this even happen? Where are the services and why are they not reaching those who need them?* That was the original 'I'm in' moment, because the standard you walk by each day is the standard you accept. I couldn't just walk by—I had to contribute to ensure a higher standard.

I personally have not experienced any struggles being a woman in this role. I mean, you've got to have thick skin in this job. This job is tough, it is demanding, and constituents do not come to see their MLA on their best days. But for me, I entered this political journey with a solid understanding and extensive background of eighteen years working with a member of Parliament. Although I was not the member for those eighteen years, I certainly was on the front line, facing everything that walked through Mr. Keddy's doors. I grew up and was taught to be strong—I come from a long line of strong women and was surrounded by three brothers. I have always believed you get what you tolerate, and I have never been one to tolerate disrespect. Of course, I have had men say to me, "Kim you have gained so much weight since being elected, is all you do sit on your rear and eat at receptions?" But really, that doesn't bother me. There will forever be people who say mean things. Sadly, the world is not kind.

I've been so blessed since starting this political journey. I've had the opportunity to become a mentor to young women in my constituency. I feel it is so important to engage our youth and give back. I always encourage our youth to become involved in their communities. Time spent helping and working with others in your communities will create a feeling of belonging, compassion, and a sense of appreciation. For me, my time volunteering in my community gave me a sense of belonging as an active citizen, and it taught me to understand the challenges people face. It increased my self confidence, gave me a sense of pride and increased my perceptions beyond just my community. It also opened doors that I never thought existed. Working with associations and boards within your community exposes you to many personalities and is an opportunity to listen and share your ideas. It is also a time to learn that just because someone does not agree with your idea or your words, they are your convictions and you should chase them. I have so enjoyed the youth that have volunteered in my office as participants of the Duke of Edinburgh program.

One of my proudest moments is a young lady who I, while campaigning, encouraged to become part of my campaign team while she was home on break from university. Our first days were spent door knocking together, then she was making calls on her own, being part of something she truly believed in—democracy and me, as her candidate. I was moved by her ambition and understanding of issues facing Nova Scotians and encouraged her to apply as an intern on Parliament Hill. In a very short time, she has worked on many campaigns and is now in the leader of the official opposition's office in Ottawa. She is twenty-two years old, and all it took was to ask her to become involved. I feel it is important to engage and empower young voices, especially young women. Be that somebody who makes everyone feel like a somebody—that's what I strive to do each day. I am also a proud mother of two very strong, independent women. As a single mother, my girls learned the value of a dollar, hard work, and that the world owes you nothing—it was here before you.

Luckily for me, I was introduced to politics at a very young age by my grandfather—a war veteran who always brought me up to make sure I knew that my voice, especially as a female, should never be silenced. And it never was. I've never been one that's at a loss for words. My grandfather was a very strong country boy, who almost fifty years ago started teaching me to be a strong female, to be bold and always have the courage to stand and say, "This is who I am." I truly believe my time spent with my grandfather, George Fancy, set me on the road to success. At a young age, we attended every Remembrance Day service together. I can still see him standing at the cenotaph with his boots freshly shined, tears running down his cheek as they played *The Last Post* and the sound of his service medals clanging in the wind. It was during this time that he silently taught me the importance of democracy and the role I needed to play. I am still driven by these memories. He had a tremendous impact on my life, and I will love him forever and miss him dearly.

Growing up in North Brookfield, a remote community in rural Nova Scotia, I can assure you my small-town roots never limited me—they inspired and strengthened me. No matter where my journey may take me, I will never forget where I came from—I will just share it with the world.

ACKNOWLEDGEMENTS

There are many people who made this project possible.

Thank you first to all the women who agreed to participate and tell us their stories. Without you, this project and the scholarship would not be possible. You made history as the first 50 women ever elected in Nova Scotia, and we hope this book serves as a reminder and a record of your accomplishments.

Thank you to Camille Horton-Poole and Abby Newcombe—fellow Daughters of the Vote. You are the embodiment of women supporting women and friends supporting friends, and your contribution to this project allowed it to begin and turn into what it is today.

Thank you to Lexi Harrington, who has edited Sarah's crazy writing since the eighth grade and leant her hand to this project. There is no better friend to have than an editor, except maybe a videographer—and with that, thank you to Will Harrington for lending his immense talent to us and creating a video for our fundraising campaign. Talk about talented siblings.

Thank you to Equal Voice and the Nova Scotia Advisory Council on the Status of Women for giving this project grant money and support. You turned a dream into a reality. As well, to the staff at the Nova Scotia Legislature including David McDonald and Peter Efthymiadis who shared their time and resources with us.

A huge thank you to Grace Lee, Emily Snooks, David Black, Leah Sarson, and Louise Carbert for aiding us in the creation of the scholarship fund that accompanies this book. Because of the hours of work you put in, young women at Dalhousie will be inspired for years to come. As well, thanks to the Dalhousie Alumni Division and the Junior League of Halifax for hosting a launch event on International Women's Day.

And thank you to our family and friends—who heard us rant, celebrate, cry and plan during this project that turned from a "we can do this in a few months" to a two-year long extravaganza.

PHOTOGRAPAHY

Some of the photographs in this book were taken by Mohammad Al of Mosy Photography. He is a local photographer originally from Syria and runs a professional photography business.

Mosy Photography can be found at www.mosyphotography.ca/

Email: info@mosyphotography.ca
Facebook: @mosyphotography
Instagram: @mosy.ca

SPONSORS

Thank you to our generous sponsors who have contributed to our book and scholarship fund. Young women will be supported for years to come because of your support.

ABOUT THE AUTHORS

SARAH DOBSON

Sarah is a graduate of the Schulich School of Law (JD '20) and Dalhousie Political Science (BA '17). She is set to complete her articling year at Cox & Palmer in Halifax, Nova Scotia and get called to the Nova Scotia Bar in June 2021. She finished law school with over ten academic awards for highest standing in courses, as well as the Judge Fran Potts Award in Law for combining academic success with a commitment to the Dalhousie Community. She also won Dalhousie's most prestigious award, a Board of Governor's award, in 2017. In 2021, she will begin a clerkship with the Nova Scotia Court of Appeal.

GRACE EVANS

Grace is a fourth-year political science student at Dalhousie and set to graduate in 2021. She has worked on several campaigns in Nova Scotia, and has devoted her time to helping women get elected across the province. Throughout her degree, Grace has worked for several MLAs and cabinet ministers, including some of the women featured in this book, in Halifax, Nova Scotia.

CPSIA information can be obtained
at www.ICGtesting.com
Printed in the USA
BVHW021333070921
615735BV00009B/3